STEP-BY-STEP GARDEN PROJECTS

Martin Walters

Gardens for Birds

Practical advice on how to attract
birds to your garden

AURA BOOKS

Step-by-Step
Garden Projects
Gardens for Birds

Martin Walters

Copyright © 2006
Advanced Marketing (UK) Ltd, Bicester, England

Produced by Transedition Limited for
Aura Books, Bicester

Typesetting:
Asgard Publishing Services, Leeds

Picture credits

Robert Dickson/Natural Image 49, 51, 56, 58, 60t;
Bob Gibbons/Natural Image 9, 21, 22, 23, 34, 45,
70t; Mike Lane/Natural Image 3, 24, 25, 41, 42,
44, 47, 50, 52t, 54t, 55, 57, 59, 63r, 64t, 65, 66b,
68t, 70b, 71, 72, 73; Mike Powles/Natural Image
39, 46; Howard Rice 2, 4, 5, 11, 12, 13, 14, 15,
16, 17, 19, 26, 30, 32, 37; Simon Stirrup 52b, 64b,
66t, 68b; Peter Wilson/Natural Image 43, 48, 53,
54b, 60b, 61, 63l

All drawings by Michael Wood

10 9 8 7 6 5 4 3 2 1

Printed in Dubai

ISBN 1 903938 85 6

Martin Walters is a writer, editor and natural-
ist. A keen birdwatcher, he also has a special
interest in plants, habitats and conservation.

Growing up in a bird-friendly botanic garden
inspired him from an early age with an
interest in the use made by wild birds of
garden plants, both native and exotic.

Martin has published regularly. His books
include field guides to birds and flowers, and
many nature reference works.

CONTENTS

4   **Introduction**
Attracting birds to your garden   4

9   **Planning the bird garden**
How to create a bird-friendly garden   9
Trees, shrubs and other plants   10
Lawns   17
Water features for birds   18

21   **Feeding garden birds**
Feeding behaviour   21
Feeding adaptations of garden birds   22
What to feed   25
Types of feeder   28
When to feed   31
Hygiene   33

34   **Garden nesting sites**
Gardens for nesting birds   34
Nest boxes   34
Nesting habits   37

40   **Directory of garden birds**
Birds by season   40
Short descriptions   40

74   **Threats and dangers**
Predators   75
Grey squirrels   75
Plate glass   76
Weather   76

77   **Useful information**
Bird organisations   77
The Garden BirdWatch Project   78
Garden bird food suppliers   78
Further reading   79

80   **Index**

Attracting birds to your garden

Interest in birds has never been higher, as membership of the bird various organizations testify. In Britain we are very lucky in having such a diverse range of habitats and reserves, excellent access to the countryside, and a long history of nature conservation. Yet our birds are also under threat, as natural habitats and traditional, low-intensity farming disappear. For this reason, the green reservoirs represented by the patchwork of parks and gardens in villages, towns, cities and their suburbs are ever more important for our birdlife, and gardens are arguably some of the richest of all the habitats available to wildlife today.

Many people are successfully re-creating 'natural' habitats in their own gardens. Lawns, for example, can be turned into flower-rich meadows by allowing the grasses and herbs to grow tall, then cutting a hay crop once or twice a year. This gives the birds a range of seeds and insects to eat, and also attracts butterflies and other useful invertebrates.

Wildlife-friendly gardening is increasingly popular, and the trend is now away from manicured, sterile lawns, clipped hedges and shrubs to gardens planned not just for the plants, but also for the benefit of birds and other wildlife. This is healthier all round, for it means using fewer chemicals such as pesticides and weedkillers – after all, in a balanced, ecological garden many pests are destroyed by their own predators, because the natural food chains of predator and prey can be maintained. This is not to say that the occasional use of artificial inputs is ruled out, but to attract birds to your garden, staying as close to nature as

Although they may make an interesting design, low-clipped plants and gravel are not the best way to attract birds to your garden.

Birds prefer a garden with a range of habitats, as here, with trees, dense shrubs and access to water.

possible is certainly the best route.

There are also things you can do specifically to attract the birds, such as providing food for the various species, particularly at times when natural food sources are scarce, and putting up nest boxes or planting cover to encourage the use of more natural nesting sites.

There are now many suppliers of bird food and a surprisingly large range of nest boxes, not just for robins and tits, but also for 'fussier' birds such as owls, house martins and even swifts. It is a great pleasure to watch birds taking food to the nest. Gardens are productive breeding sites for a number of birds, many of which have invaded gardens from their original woodland or hedgerow habitats.

There are birds that we instantly associate with gardens – blackbird, song thrush, robin, house sparrow, great and blue tits, for example - and few gardens are without some or all of these regulars. But the habits of wild birds do change, as do their populations, and while some once common species, such as spotted flycatcher, have virtually vanished from our gardens and from the wider countryside, others, including green woodpecker and black-cap, are now seen more and more often. Even the sly and

stately grey heron can often be spotted gliding and spiralling down to a garden pond, especially in the early hours of the morning, and particularly if the pond is stocked with juicy fish!

Newcomers are not always welcomed, though, and this is probably true of the many

magpies which have invaded suburban gardens in recent years - but all these add to the variety of our garden birds, and each species is interesting in its own way.

Although pressures on garden birds seem high – from domestic cats and magpies, for example -

Key points

Points to bear in mind for increasing the number and range of birds in your garden:

- Create diverse habitats.
- Avoid or minimise the use of chemicals.
- Offer a choice of healthy food.
- Provide attractive sites for nesting, including nest boxes.

in fact gardens are highly productive, supporting large numbers of birds despite the activities of these predators, and they usually offer relatively safe nesting sites. Losses, especially of young birds, to predators such as squirrels, crows, magpies and sparrowhawks are sometimes high and can be distressing, but there is actually little evidence that they reduce urban and suburban populations of songbirds. The birds just seem to produce more offspring and make up the losses. The presence of sparrowhawks, for example, is in fact evidence for the existence of a healthy food chain, from garden invertebrates, through songbirds, to the hawks themselves. The latter are small in number in the garden ecosystem, although they may occasionally make dramatic appearances.

Domestic cats may be a bigger problem in some gardens,

especially in terraces with narrow gardens, where the density of cats can also be particularly high. Cats are not natural enemies of our native birds, which are therefore rather vulnerable to them, and some cats certainly do take large numbers of garden birds, especially fledglings of species such as blackbirds.

This book is an introductory guide to point you towards making your garden as bird-friendly as possible. For identifying garden birds there are many other books available, and this book should be used in conjunction with established identification guides.

The first section explains the basic steps needed to plan a garden that is attractive to wild birds, showing how to create a variety of habitats within the space available, and suggesting a choice of bird-friendly species of trees, shrubs and other plants, both native and exotic.

The next section looks at the provision of food for garden birds. The range of feeders, tables and other equipment for

garden birds is now extensive, as is the variety of food available through garden centres and specialist suppliers.

We can also encourage birds to nest in our gardens, both by providing 'natural' sites such as suitable trees and cover, and also by using a range of nest boxes. This aspect is covered in the subsequent section.

The main section is a species-by-species directory highlighting those birds which are most likely to be seen in gardens. The species are arranged in systematic sequence so that related birds are close together for ease of comparison and identification. The commonest species are indicated with an asterisk, and we have also shown whether the species is resident (found throughout the year), or a summer or winter visitor. Each entry contains sections on the bird's food preferences, its preferred habitats, behaviour and status.

Advantages of a bird-friendly garden

Nearly all gardens, whether they be large or tiny, can be made more attractive to wild birds. This will help to make the garden a more fascinating and welcoming environment, as well as helping to conserve the birds themselves. Moreover, a healthy bird population will also help to reduce harmful insects and other pests in the garden, thus reducing the need to rely on chemical weedkillers or pesticides.

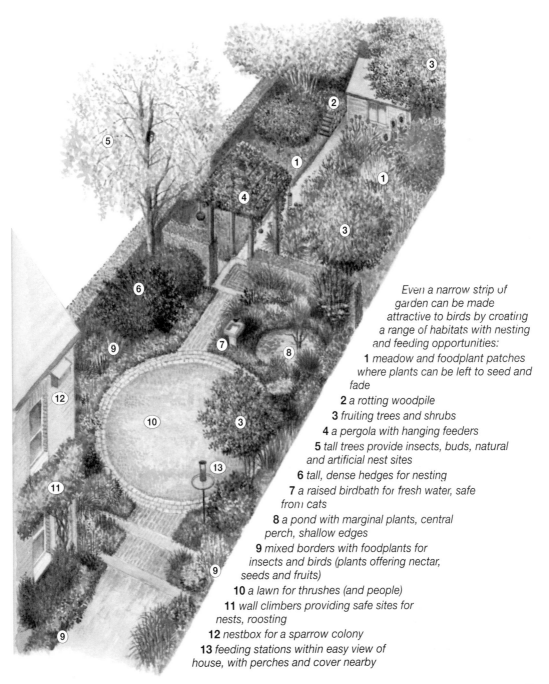

Even a narrow strip of garden can be made attractive to birds by creating a range of habitats with nesting and feeding opportunities:

1 *meadow and foodplant patches where plants can be left to seed and fade*

2 *a rotting woodpile*

3 *fruiting trees and shrubs*

4 *a pergola with hanging feeders*

5 *tall trees provide insects, buds, natural and artificial nest sites*

6 *tall, dense hedges for nesting*

7 *a raised birdbath for fresh water, safe from cats*

8 *a pond with marginal plants, central perch, shallow edges*

9 *mixed borders with foodplants for insects and birds (plants offering nectar, seeds and fruits)*

10 *a lawn for thrushes (and people)*

11 *wall climbers providing safe sites for nests, roosting*

12 *nestbox for a sparrow colony*

13 *feeding stations within easy view of house, with perches and cover nearby*

A larger garden such as this one provides countless opportunities for creating a very bird-friendly environment:

1 a meandering area of lawn
2 mixed borders
3 a large, naturalistic pond
4 fruiting trees, e.g. crab apple, cherry, rowan
5 a carefully placed birdbath and feeding stations offering different foods
6 meadow areas and tall perennials for flowers and seeds
7 shrubby thickets and a tall boundary hedge providing secure nest sites
8 a large tree with an owl box

How to create a bird-friendly garden

Always try and think from the birds' point of view:

- Is there enough food?

- Are there plenty of safe nesting opportunities provided?

- Is the garden free from damaging chemicals?

The essential technique for creating a bird-friendly garden is to offer a range of feeding sites, combined with adequate cover – ideally in an environment that is safe from predators.

Whilst it is true that birds enjoy 'wild' gardens, it is quite possible to attract a wide range of birds to more conventional, managed gardens while retaining their horticultural interest as well. In fact, a managed garden with a multitude of habitats – such as an open lawn, herbaceous borders, shrubberies and tall trees, and ideally a pond – is likely to have a richer bird life than an old garden that has been allowed to run wild and revert to nature.

That said, incorporating a 'wild' section into the overall garden design will certainly benefit the wildlife, birds included, and add to the diversity. It is not only the birds that will benefit either: there will also be more insects, including butterflies, and hedgehogs will probably also be encouraged to take up residence in your garden. The latter are the gardeners' friend, keeping down the numbers of harmful slugs.

Food provision is not just a case of bird tables and feeding stations, since most birds rely more on natural sources such as insects, worms, molluscs and other invertebrates for their basic diet, at least in the spring and summer. Feeding is most important in cold weather when natural supplies are scarce, although with the range of foods available now, feeding at other seasons is also desirable, and the advice nowadays is that birds will appreciate supplementary feeding throughout the year – provided that suitable food is offered.

Rather than remove pests with chemical sprays, it is surely better to let their natural enemies, the birds, thrive, and simultaneously do this job for you. A bird-rich garden need not be an untidy garden, as long as it offers both variety and rich

Garlic mustard (Alliaria petiolata) *can be encouraged to grow in a rough corner of the garden, and will encourage insects, including orange-tip butterflies.*

sources of nutrition.

Having said that, an untidy corner – perhaps a pile of rotting logs hidden near a compost heap, for example – will boost the invertebrate food supply and be appreciated by the birds. Providing such habitats is a splendid way to encourage beetles, woodlice, spiders and many other invertebrates. These will do no damage to your garden, but will certainly benefit the birds.

Not surprisingly, native weeds are more likely to be suitable as a food source for our native birds, and the weeds will also harbour the insects and other small creatures that are the natural prey of birds. Indigenous

A pile of logs left to decay will create a micro-habitat rich in invertebrates, which in turn will provide food for many garden birds.

 ### Windows

Large windows, especially where light shines through from windows on the opposite side of the house, can be a death trap for birds, as they are sometimes killed trying to fly through what seems to them to be open space.

You can prevent this by sticking silhouettes of birds to the offending windows (see page 76). There is even some evidence that hawk cut-outs are particularly effective, as most songbirds instinctively avoid such outlines.

insects, such as bees and butterflies, will also benefit, and these will enhance the garden in their own right, as well as providing further food sources for the birds. In short, try and think 'natural ecosystems and food chains' and you will be on the right track.

Another good tip is to leave plants that have finished flowering to go to seed naturally, rather than dead-heading them or grubbing up fruiting annuals. This way the seeds will remain on the stems, to the benefit of many seed-eating birds. The plants can always be tidied up

later when the birds have had their fill. Windfall or ripe fruits can be left on the ground where they drop, and will be welcomed by many garden birds such as starlings, blackbirds and thrushes.

Trees, shrubs and other plants

Birds are mostly rather shy creatures, and many species rely on hiding in amongst shrubs and other vegetation to escape detection. For this reason a bird-friendly garden needs to have adequate cover, and trees and shrubs are very important.

The fruits of the crabapple tree are too sour for human tastes, but are eagerly eaten by many garden birds.

Think about the changing seasons. There will need to be adequate cover for the birds even when the deciduous species have lost their leaves. A good mixture of deciduous and evergreen species is therefore recommended. The latter offer cover even in winter, and are sometimes chosen as safe roosting sites.

If you are lucky enough to have old established trees in your garden, try to resist the temptation to fell them (you may need special permission to do so in any case). Old trees tend to have natural holes and nooks, which may be exploited as nesting sites (see page 38). Tree trunks are also good places for attaching nest boxes.

As well as providing cover, trees and shrubs are also an excellent food source for birds, either directly from the plant, as seeds or fruits, or indirectly through the invertebrates they support. A mature tree such as a birch or willow can be host to hundreds of different kinds of insects and spiders, most of which will provide food for insectivorous birds.

Always remember that native trees and shrubs will provide more food than will exotic, imported species. Examples of good native trees are oak, ash, beech, birch, alder and willow; gardens with the native species

of these trees will benefit from a good supply of caterpillars and other insects, spiders and other invertebrates, as well as the seeds, cones and nuts from the trees themselves.

Berries are an important and nutritious food for garden birds, and many native and exotic shrubs produce edible fruits which are attractive to birds. The berry season stretches from late summer through autumn and well into the winter, with different species fruiting at different times. This means that with careful planting you can ensure that a whole range of berries is on offer during the months when other food sources are relatively scarce.

Native plants

The native species listed overleaf (mainly trees and shrubs) are particularly useful, and will help to attract birds. Some, such

 Suitable plants

The pages that follow contain some native and non-native species that are commonly available and that are particularly suitable for the bird garden, whether for the cover they offer or as a food source – or in many cases both.

Trees are highlighted with a **T** after their name, and shrubs with an **S**.

as the larger trees, offer safe feeding sites, while others provide dense foliage for nesting. Many support good numbers of edible insects and their larvae, and some have tasty

11

berries. Since they are all familiar to our native birds, these plants tend to act as magnets to bring the birds into the garden.

Alder T
Alnus glutinosa
This tree grows quickly in damp soil, to a maximum of around 20 m (65 ft). It is especially suitable for waterlogged sites, such as around larger ponds or alongside streams. The alder produces catkins and cones, which are attractive to finches such as goldfinch, redpoll and siskin, as well as to tits.

Ash T
Fraxinus excelsior
Ash is best suited to chalky or limestone soils, and will in time grow to over 25 m (80 ft). This attractive tree has divided leaves so that it casts a light shadow. It provides excellent singing perches, and the trunk is a good site for nest boxes.

Beech T
Fagus sylvatica
One of our most beautiful trees, potentially growing to 40 m (130 ft). It has a smooth grey bark and fine autumn colours. The fruits, known as beech mast, are abundant in some years and are eaten by many birds, notably finches, woodpeckers and nuthatches. Beech can also be pruned to create a hedge, in which case the leaves tend to remain on the twigs for much longer.

Birch T
Betula pubescens,
B. pendula
These are rather small trees, growing to about 20 m (65 ft). They grow best on somewhat acid sandy or peaty soils, and are useful in smaller as well as large gardens. The birch supports a good range of insects, and also produces catkins. It is favoured by warblers, finches and tits.

Bramble S
Rubus fruticosus
Brambles form a highly variable group of deciduous or semi-evergreen shrubs, mostly with sharp prickles and rambling growth. They are very good for providing cover for nesting birds, and of course also produce edible fruits (blackberries) in the autumn, which are eaten particularly by thrushes, black-birds, redwings and fieldfares, as well as by people.

Sea buckthorn S
Hippophae rhamnoides
The main natural habitat of this shrub is coastal dunes. Yet it is suitable for the garden, being drought-resistant. It thrives best on light, sandy soils. Sea buck-thorn produces edible orange berries that are eaten by birds such as thrushes and their relatives.

Bird cherry T/S
Prunus padus
A small tree or shrub with pretty white flowers and small, sour cherry fruits. It hosts many edible insects, and the fruits are eaten by birds.

Wild cherry T
Prunus avium
The wild cherry is larger than the previous species. It is a woodland plant, and is similarly a rich source of insects and fruits.

The berries of holly are a particular favourite of wintering migrants such as redwings and fieldfares.

Crabapple T
Malus sylvestris
Crabapple is a small, densely branched tree, usually less than 8 m (25 ft) tall, with small apples that ripen in late autumn and winter (see photo on page 11). The tree hosts rich insect life and the apples are readily eaten by birds.

Elder S/T
Sambucus nigra
This native shrub or small tree provides good cover for roosting or nesting. It also has attractive flat-topped clusters of aromatic creamy flowers (used for elderflower cordial and wine), which turn into glossy black berries with a deep-red juice in late summer and autumn. Many birds feed on the berries.

Guelder-rose S
Viburnum opulus
This shrub grows best on slightly damp soils, and will produce suckers from the roots. The translucent red berries, which are produced in September and October, are relished by many birds.

Hawthorn S/T
Crataegus monogyna
The hawthorn is a shrub or small tree that is very familiar from our woods and hedgerows, and it grows well in the garden too. Native birds like to nest amongst the dense branches and twigs, whose thorns offer good protection. The bright-red berries, which appear from the autumn through the winter, are eaten by thrushes, woodpigeons and many other birds.

Hazel S/T
Corylus avellana
Common as an understorey shrub in our native woods, hazel is useful in the garden as well. Although hazel nuts are mainly attractive to squirrels and other rodents (including dormice in some areas), hazels also offer good cover and insect life.

Holly S/T
Ilex aquifolium
One of the best of our native plants for the bird-friendly garden, holly can grow to quite a tall tree – 15 m (50 ft) or more – but is usually rather smaller. Holly is full of insects and spiders, and the red berries (see opposite) are taken by a wide range of birds such as thrushes (including redwings and fieldfares) and wintering blackcaps. Holly berries form in the summer, and stay on the tree a long time (unless stripped by hungry flocks), sometimes right through the winter. The spiny foliage also makes holly a good choice for nesting cover.

Honeysuckle S
Lonicera periclymenum
This popular climbing shrub looks good in most gardens, with its attractive, fragrant flowers. Dense growths of honeysuckle form excellent nesting sites for many garden birds, and the juicy berries are eaten by many species.

Hornbeam T
Carpinus betulus
This large forest tree can also be grown as a hedge, which like beech will retain its leaves in the winter if kept regularly trimmed. As a hedge, hornbeam offers good nesting sites.

Ivy S
Hedera helix
This well-known climber is a splendid addition to the bird garden, and often appears of its own accord. While a strong growth of ivy on a favoured tree can smother it, in fact ivy is no

Ivy provides evergreen cover, and nesting sites, and its berries offer winter food for birds such as blackbirds and blackcaps.

13

It is a good idea to leave the fruits (hips) on rose bushes, as these will attract the birds.

parasite, and only weakens the supporting tree by competing for light. Indeed, ivy stems on trees can be desirable as they offer a multitude of nesting platforms, and the evergreen foliage adds colour to the garden in winter. Ivy berries are eaten by many birds, including thrushes, robins, warblers (especially blackcaps) and woodpigeons. The berries are borne throughout the winter and thus provide welcome energy when other sources are in short supply.

Oak T
Quercus robur
This large, deciduous forest and woodland tree grows to about 30 m (100 ft). A mature oak is an entire ecosystem in minia-ture, providing a home to countless insects and other invertebrates. Caterpillars are often abundant in oak foliage and form food for many garden birds in spring and early summer, while the autumn acorns are welcomed by jays, woodpeckers and nuthatches. Natural holes offer nest sites to many species, including owls and kestrels (see page 38).

The rowan is a pretty tree which looks splendid in any garden. Its juicy edible fruits ripen in the autumn.

Scots pine T
Pinus sylvestris
Conifers provide welcome all-year foliage and safe roosting sites for many garden birds, notably tawny owls. The native Scots pine grows best on acid, nutrient-poor soils. Other garden birds that like conifers such as this are goldcrests, coal tits and nuthatches.

Wild rose S
Rosa species
With their delicate white or pink flowers, native roses are an attractive addition to the garden, and their tasty fruits (hips) are eaten by many birds. Rose bushes, being tangled and thorny, make good safe nesting sites.

Rowan T
Sorbus aucuparia
This very pretty small tree, often misleadingly known as the mountain ash, would look good in almost any garden, with its feathery foliage and clusters of creamy-white flowers, followed by the berries, which turn a bright scarlet when ripe. Many birds eat the berries, especially members of the thrush family.

Teasel
Dipsacus fullonum
The rigid fruiting heads of the teasel contain large numbers of tiny seeds that are especially attractive to goldfinches. Ripe seedheads can be cut and tied to the bird table or a similar site. These will often attract flocks of goldfinches. When the seeds have all been eaten, the teasel

heads can be topped up again using niger seed – a tasty substitute for the original (see page 26).

Thistle
Cirsium species, *Carduus* species
Thistles may look scruffy, but they certainly attract the birds – mainly goldfinches, linnets and the like - if left to set seed.

Traveller's joy S
Clematis vitalba
This pretty climber, also known as old man's beard, thrives on alkaline soils, and has attractive wispy, plumed fruits. Old-growth traveller's joy can form dense tangles, offering safe nesting sites.

Wayfaring tree S
Viburnum lantana
This is one of our most attractive native shrubs, growing best in chalky soils. It forms umbels of creamy-white flowers followed by red berries that ripen to black. The latter are eaten by many birds.

Willow T
Salix species
Several native willows are useful as garden plants, especially for damp sites such as near to a pond. They have a rich insect life, and also develop catkins.

Yew T
Taxus baccata
Often planted in churchyards, yew is also very suitable in a wildlife garden. Its shady evergreen foliage attracts many species, such as goldcrests and coal tits, and provides safe roosting sites for tawny owls and other birds. The bright-red fruits are eaten by many species, the poisonous seeds passing straight through without harming the birds.

The firethorn is well named for its fiery red fruits and spiny twigs. This useful shrub can be pruned and trained against a wall, offering good nesting opportunities as well as edible berries.

Sunflowers brighten up the garden, and also produce nutritious seeds welcomed by many garden birds.

Non-native plants

There are many non-native plants that benefit the birds and other wildlife in the garden. Many of these also produce attractive flowers and foliage. Here are some of the most useful.

Cotoneaster S
Cotoneaster species

These pretty shrubs produce edible red berries in the autumn, which are eaten by thrushes, including redwings and fieldfares, and also by waxwings.

Lawson cypress T
e.g. *Chamaecyparis lawsoniana*

This tree is useful for evergreen cover, and for nesting and roosting sites; it can also be trimmed to form a hedge. Roosting birds include greenfinches, starlings, collared doves and woodpigeons.

Firethorn S
Pyracantha species

This is another good berry-bearing shrub (see previous page). The twigs are thorny, so the plants also offer a relatively safe retreat for birds.

Goldenrod
Solidago canadensis

This pretty late-flowering perennial with yellow panicles produces seedheads that small finches find quite tasty.

Hydrangea petiolaris S

This climber produces pretty white flower clusters. Well-grown specimens have twisting stems which offer possible nest sites for birds.

Michaelmas daisy
Aster species

The beautiful flowers in late summer attract butterflies, hoverflies, bees, and many other insects, and in turn bring in live food for birds.

Sunflower
Helianthus annuus

The cheerful flower heads of the sunflower produce a large number of seeds that are eagerly eaten by a wide range of birds, especially finches. Many varieties are available, including giant forms.

Wisteria S
Wisteria sinensis

This climber with its beautiful scented purple or white flowers creates splendid nooks and crannies for nesting, as well as attracting insects. The stout, twisting stems form sturdy plinths for many garden birds, including the now rather uncommon spotted flycatcher.

If you have a large expanse of lawn, try leaving patches of grass unmown to encourage meadow flowers and insect life.

Lawns

Lawns are a very desirable feature in the bird-friendly garden. Not only do they look good while being easy to maintain, but many birds feed directly at or just under the lawn surface.

Blackbirds and other thrushes run across the lawn, listening for the faint rustles that indicate the presence of a juicy worm or grub just below the surface, then plunge their bills into the soil to capture their prey. Pied wagtails employ a different method – dashing forward or flitting up to seize an insect as it flies up from the grass. Starlings are also adept lawn feeders, enlarging holes by opening their beaks under the surface as they search.

One of the finest sights is that of a green woodpecker as it jumps and walks about the lawn in its hunt for ants. When they find a suitably ant-rich lawn, green woodpeckers often learn quickly which are the best hunting patches and return repeatedly to the same areas, offering good views of what is normally a shy and elusive bird.

A meadow

Part of the grassed area can be allowed to grow tall and thus develop into a meadow. Cut it just a couple of times a year, or more, depending on its lushness and rate of growth, and it will

Weedkillers

Try not to use weedkillers on your lawn, as they will reduce the food available to the birds. Regular mowing – though not too close – will help maintain a reasonable sward, and the occasional weed such as a daisy or dandelion will brighten the lawn; the latter will also provide seed for some birds.

add an extra dimension to the garden, supporting pretty grassland flowers such as ox-eye

In a larger garden, part of the lawn can be turned into a flowery meadow that will attract butterflies and other insects. These in turn will attract many birds such as spotted flycatchers and swallows.

page 20 shows all the important features of a bird-friendly pond.

Ponds can be made from concrete or (more often these days) from thick, heavy-duty synthetic liner, or they may be preformed in various shapes from glass fibre or thick plastic. Preformed ponds need even support from the soil beneath, so you need to contour the soil carefully to fit the shape. Otherwise the weight of the water can cause cracks or buckles to develop in time. When using a flexible pool liner, do ensure that the hole you dig has a covering of fine sand, and that there are no sharp objects such as flints which might puncture

daisy, buttercups, scabious and clovers. A meadow will also attract butterflies and other insects into the garden and provide an extra habitat for the birds. Many seed suppliers now offer special flower mixtures for use in garden meadows.

Water features for birds
It is not always appreciated that birds need access to water at all seasons – most obviously in hot summer weather, but also during hard frosty weather when natural sources may be iced over. They may drink from a bird bath or puddle on a hot summer's day, but many birds also bathe regularly, even in cool or cold weather, in order to help keep their feathers clean and rid themselves of dust or mites.

A birdbath
Many designs of birdbath are available. A birdbath should be placed in an open part of the garden so that the birds have a good all-round view, and are thus able to keep an eye out for potential predators.

Change the water regularly, and never allow it to get stagnant or fouled. In winter, water should be kept free of ice, not by adding anything to the water, but by regularly breaking and removing the ice from the surface.

A garden pond
If you have enough room, a garden pond is an excellent feature, allowing a greater range of plants to be grown, and also bringing in more wildlife, including birds. The picture on

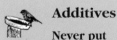 **Additives**

Never put additives in the water. Salt or glycerine will certainly help to stop it freezing, but can also cause serious problems when it gets into the birds' plumage! Simply remove the ice each day and fill the bath in the morning with warm (not boiling) water.

the liner when the pond is filled.

If small children have access to the pond, make sure that they are supervised. It is best, both for safety and for the birds, to make the pond edges slope gently, thus giving access to shallow water from which the birds can drink and bathe. Try to arrange for the shallow bathing spots to be sited away from dense fringing cover, as birds are very vulnerable when drinking or washing their plumage. Overhanging trees can be a real nuisance too, as fallen leaves quickly cause problems by clogging and decaying in the water.

When planting the pond it is best to do so rather sparsely, as some species can rapidly fill the shallow water and dominate, creating a marsh and obliterating the open water that is so

A miniature pond can be created from a half barrel, and birds will often come down to drink from water features such as this.

vital to the birds. Water plants will thrive best and oxygenate the pond if they have full light. Underwater plants, such as hornwort (*Ceratophyllum*), water violet (*Hottonia palustris*) and water milfoil (*Myriophyllum*), and floating aquatics such as water lilies (e.g. *Nymphaea* and *Nuphar*) can be bought and planted, and should become established quite quickly

If your pond is stocked with goldfish or ornamental carp, remember that these can be a very tempting target for herons. It is often better to allow native aquatic animals to populate the pond naturally, and it is surprising how quickly this can

Running water adds interest to the garden and is also attractive to birds.

happen – water snails, pond skaters, water boatmen, water beetles, newts and frogs all usually appear in due course.

A fountain
Prefabricated bubble fountain units are available, consisting of a hidden reservoir to set below ground and a circulating pump to issue water from a drilled rock or other feature. A shallow dish or liner may be placed beneath the cobbles on the perforated cover of the reservoir, to collect enough water for drinking and bathing. The result is a water feature that is safe for children and attractive to birds.

If you have room to make a pond for birds, choose an irregular shape with varied depths of water. Provide plenty of fringing vegetation, but also allow some more open shallow spots where birds can bathe in safety.

1 *A gently sloping bank of pebbles and gravel gives birds access to shallow water for bathing, and offers an escape route for hedgehogs.*

2 *A branch provides a safe perch from which small birds can drink.*

3 *A mixture of submerged, emergent and marginal plants helps to aerate the water and support a range of pond life.*

4 *Rocks and old logs can provide cover for wildlife.*

5 *A separate bog garden provides a home for more vigorous marginal plants that would choke a small pond.*

6 *A top-up water supply can be directed from a water butt.*

7 *Nearby trees provide cover without overhanging the pond.*

8 *A bridge or deck provides a viewing point.*

Feeding garden birds

Feeding behaviour

Observing the behaviour of garden birds is a rewarding activity in its own right, and it also helps us to understand their feeding requirements. Different species use diffcrent areas in the garden, and it is fascinating to watch how they exploit these various niches.

Some species such as wren and dunnock tend to flit about at low levels, often amongst the undergrowth or on the ground, while tits are generally seen amongst the branches of trees or shrubs. Blackbirds and thrushes, and also green wood-pcckers, favour the open expanses offered by lawns, watching warily for danger as they systematically probe the surface for tasty invertebrates.

Small finches, such as gold-finches and linnets, often form flocks as they feed on the seedheads of herbs, including thistles and teasel. The larger finches – chaffinches and

Small tortoiseshells are one of the commoner garden butterflies. An insect-friendly garden is usually also bird-friendly.

greenfinches – like to fly fairly high in the trees, but also make good use of bird tables and hanging feeders; greenfinches are especially fond of peanuts.

Other garden birds generally prefer to stick to the safety of the trees – for example, coal tits and goldcrests. The same is true to a lesser extent of nuthatches and the spotted woodpeckers, although great spotted wood-peckers and nuthatches may be tempted to feeding stations, especially in cold weather. When coal tits use a feeder, they tend to extract tiny items of

Some garden birds can become quite tame, though it is unusual for a song thrush to feed from the hand!

Two of these frosted rose hips show clear signs of having been pecked at by grateful birds.

food, one at a time, taking each of them back to (typically) a coniferous tree before feeding.

Treecreepers are specialist bark feeders, and whilst they may be present in larger gardens, rarely come to bird tables or feeders, preferring to hunt amongst the cracks of tree trunks.

Starlings are truly all-purpose birds, making use of a huge range of feeding opportunities and sites, from open lawns to aerial insects, as well as swooping greedily on all sorts of scraps and other food at bird tables and hanging feeders.

Great tits, and even more so blue tits, are highly acrobatic. They find hanging feeders perfect, and are usually among the first garden birds to make use of them. Some garden birds – notably the sadly now rather uncommon spotted flycatcher – find gardens to their liking, but don't make use of the extra food offered, preferring to stick rigidly to their diet of flying insects. Other birds, such as swallows, house martins and swifts, feed only in the air, either swooping low over gardens and fields, or high in the sky, often (mainly swifts) so high that they are almost invisible.

Feeding garden birds undoubtedly helps them build up their numbers and survive periods of inclement weather. It also brings them closer to us, allowing much better views, and opportunities to learn about their habits.

Feeding adaptations of garden birds

The different types of garden birds are adapted to using different sources of food. Some specialise on invertebrates, especially insects, while others are mainly seed eaters, and others again are able to exploit a wide range of foods.

Insect eaters

Birds adapted to feeding mainly on insect prey, or on similar small invertebrates, tend to have thin bills and a slim and rather agile build. Examples are warblers such as blackcap, garden warbler, willow warbler and chiffchaff, but also goldcrest, wren and treecreeper. These birds find most of their food in the foliage or bark of trees and shrubs.

The spotted flycatcher is one of the most specialised of all insectivores, using its acrobatic antics to pluck flying insects from mid-air.

Woodpeckers use another technique, patrolling the bark of tree-trunks and probing with their chisel-like bills below the bark for grubs such as beetle larvae. Green woodpeckers also gobble up ants in enormous quantities from meadows and lawns, using their long tongues. Wrens hunt in tangled undergrowth for insects and spiders, while tiny goldcrests flit for similar prey amongst the twigs of conifers.

Many insectivorous birds switch to eating berries or other fruits during autumn and winter. Winter berry-feeders include thrushes and blackbirds, fieldfares and redwings, but also blackcaps, and those rare or irregular visitors, the waxwings.

Song thrushes and snails

One of the most remarkable behaviours among familiar garden birds is the way that song thrushes eat snails. Although snails are not actually their staple diet, they use them as a back-up food if other food sources are scarce.

A song thrush picks up a snail, and then repeatedly knocks it against a stone or other hard surface until the shell breaks, before gobbling up the soft body (see photo on page 57).

Seed eaters

Finches, sparrows and buntings are predominantly seed eaters. Their bills are rather short, deep and strong, and are well able to crush hard seed coats.

House sparrows prefer grain, and have followed people and agriculture in many countries across the globe; they will also take peanuts. Fewer stubble fields with grain in winter may well be a significant factor in their recent decline. Tree sparrows, however, prefer the seeds of weed species rather than wheat grain.

Greenfinches have sturdy bills which can cope with a wide range of seeds. They are very nimble and agile, and are amongst the first garden birds to appear at hanging seed feeders, peanuts and black sunflower

seeds being particular favourites. They are also partial to rose hips, so it is worth leaving some fruiting heads on rose bushes for them to enjoy.

Chaffinches are also mainly seed eaters, although they are not as acrobatic as sparrows and greenfinches, preferring to seek their food on the ground. Bullfinches are notorious for their fondness for buds, including those of fruit trees, which they eat towards the end of

The seeds of teasel are a favourite food of goldfinches. The dead fruiting plants can also be bunched and tied to a post or bird table.

Though normally shy and elusive, nuthatches do sometimes visit bird tables.

winter. They also enjoy feeding on ash keys and the seeds of honesty, and will take black sunflower seed as well. The shy and local hawfinch has the biggest bill of all our finches, and its strong mandibles can even crack open cherry stones.

Goldfinches, linnets, siskins and redpolls have short, somewhat pointed bills, and can extract tiny seeds from thistles and other plants, and from the cones of birch and alder trees. Goldfinches love the seeds of teasel, so it is worth planting a patch of teasel especially for these beautiful finches. They also like black sunflower seeds and will quickly learn to come to feeders stocked with this food. Their relative the siskin is a more elusive seed eater. With its sharply pointed bill, it is adept at extracting seeds from the cones of pines, and also alder. Siskins also sometimes come to peanut feeders, mainly in the winter.

Yellowhammers and reed buntings are the only buntings that appear in gardens with any frequency, usually in winter.

Yellowhammers flock to open fields in the winter and they can sometimes be enticed into the garden in frosty weather. They are fond of grain and also sunflower hearts. Reed buntings occasionally turn up, and may feed on sunflower seeds.

The tits are rather unusual feeders. Although naturally mainly insectivorous, they are also very keen on food provided at bird tables and feeders, especially peanuts. Blue tits and great tits are ever-present at peanut feeders. Coal tits and marsh tits like black sunflower seeds and often carry away individual seeds to hoard or else to eat within the safety of the trees.

A dish fixed to the top of a pole makes a simple but effective feeding station.

Dangling nut feeders beneath a bird table gives more space for aggressive species like these blue tits to feed simultaneously.

Generalist feeders

Several garden birds are genuine all-rounders when it comes to feeding.

Members of the crow family – jackdaws, jays, magpies, rooks and carrion/hooded crows – are able to feed on almost anything. Jays, which we tend to associate with acorns, will feed on beech mast, peanuts, kitchen scraps, and even snails and mealworms. Rooks flock to fields to search for worms and grubs. In colder weather they may also forage for grain, potatoes and beet, which often makes them unpopular with farmers. Rooks will also come into gardens for scraps from time to time.

Starlings are also true generalists when it comes to feeding, their all-purpose bills being suitable for exploiting a huge range of different food sources.

What to feed – natural food, extra food

One of the most obvious ways in which we can attract birds into our gardens is by offering them food. This can be done by planting tree species that produce edible fruits or seeds, especially if these are native plants familiar to our birds (see pages 12–16 for some suitable trees, shrubs and other plants).

However, perhaps the most obvious way is to provide extra food, and there are now many types of bird-feeding equipment available, as well as an almost bewildering range of different foods on offer.

Pure seeds or fruits

Peanuts are very popular for feeding to many different species of garden birds – notably house sparrows and greenfinches, as well as great,

blue, long-tailed and coal tits.

Peanuts are a high-energy food rich in oils and proteins, and are therefore very suitable as winter food, although they may be offered throughout the year. Most suppliers will offer 'afla-toxin-tested' peanuts, which are free from the poison that can sometimes develop in these nuts, produced by fungal attack on mouldy peanuts. Feeders and stored peanuts should be checked regularly, and discarded if there are signs of mould developing.

Peanuts can also be bought as granules, which are acceptable to a wider range of birds and pose no danger of choking to nestlings. Peanuts that have been roasted or salted should not be offered.

Sunflower seeds can be purchased whole or as sunflower hearts with the husks removed. Black

sunflower seeds are particularly rich in oil and also have a thinner seed coat, which makes them suitable for a wider range of species.

Vine fruits. Sultanas, currants and raisins are excellent food for so-called 'softbill' species such as robins, blackbirds and thrushes. They are usually best offered after soaking, which makes them more palatable.

Niger seed is the name of a very fine, oil-rich seed that has only recently become available. It comes from a tropical plant (*Guizotia abyssinica*) related to the sunflower that is native to Ethiopia. Niger seed is rich in oils, making it a good source of energy for small seed eaters. It is very popular with small finches, especially goldfinches and siskins.

You can either use a special niger seed feeder or top up the fruiting heads of teasel (see page 23) with these tiny seeds, which are similar in size to thistle seed.

Seed mixtures

Many different blends of mixed seeds are available, including sunflower seed (with or without husks), millet, hemp, flaked maize and peanuts (also as granules). Some mixtures also have dried berries and other fruits incorporated, and even insects such as dried mealworms. Experimenting with seed mixtures will soon tell you which are most popular in your own garden. There are also special grain mixtures for ducks, geese and swans.

Some mixtures contain pulses such as peas, beans and lentils, but these should be avoided, as they are unsuitable for most smaller garden birds. Mixtures with small seeds such as millet are good for finches, dunnocks and sparrows.

Live foods

Mealworms (flour beetle larvae) are probably the most popular live food, and these are greedily eaten by many birds, including robins, blackbirds

Robins come readily to feed at bird tables, especially during cold winter weather.

Breeding mealworms

Mealworms are easy to rear for yourself. Simply put bran into a large container and 'seed' it with mealworms. These will hatch into adult flour beetles, which will breed in the bran and produce a new crop of larvae - the 'worms'.

and thrushes. They can also be bought dried. Waxworms (wax moth larvae) are also sometimes available. Ant 'eggs' (actually the pupae) can be bought at some pet shops. These are mainly sold for cage birds, but are equally good for feeding wild species. Insects are highly nutritious and are appreciated by many birds, especially for feeding to their young in the nest.

Although maggots (blowfly larvae) are widely available from fishing suppliers, and are readily eaten by many birds, they are not suitable because they have been suspected of causing salmonella poisoning in birds.

Fat foods

Cakes and balls made from suet can be bought in various shapes and sizes, and are an excellent food for garden birds in the winter. The fat matrix usually contains additives such as finely ground nuts, fruits and even insects. These may be hung directly from twigs or a bird table, or placed inside metal mesh baskets. Suet is also available in pellet form. Many wild birds, including more unusual species such as nuthatches and woodpeckers, find these fat balls irresistible.

Some fat balls are sold in nylon mesh bags. In this case the balls should be removed from the bags before being offered to the birds, as there is the danger of entanglement. Songbirds have delicate feet with thin toes, and they sometimes panic if their feet get snagged, resulting in injury, or worse.

Household scraps

Many kitchen scraps are suitable for feeding to wild birds. Dried fruits are useful, especially sultanas, currants and raisins, as are fresh fruits such as apples and pears, which are best cut into small pieces. Bruised or slightly rotten apples can be offered to the birds rather than being thrown away or composted. Grated cheese is favoured by robins, thrushes, blackbirds and dunnocks.

Potatoes are another good source of nourishment - especially cold baked potatoes, which should be split open. Bread is also suitable, especially wholemeal bread, though this should not be the main food offered, as most bread (particularly white bread) has rather low nutritional value. Pastry is much better, as is cooked rice, and porridge oats.

Robins and tits like bacon, especially fatty bacon, and this can be hung from a string or chopped up into small pieces. Cat food and dog food are also welcomed by birds, but don't offer dry dog biscuits.

Fresh coconut will attract blue tits and great tits in particular, and is very nutritious; but never use desiccated coconut, as this can expand in the bird's stomach and cause digestive problems. A split coconut shell can be used again as a fat container after the birds have eaten the coconut flesh itself.

Home-made bird cake

You can easily make your own bird cake using either suet or lard:

- Take a suitable container such as half a coconut shell, a ceramic bell or a similar receptacle.

- Fill it with edible foods such as a mixture of seeds, oatmeal, dried fruits and cheese.

- Pour melted fat over the mixture and leave it to cool and set.

Types of feeder

A glance through any wildlife supplier catalogue or natural history magazine will reveal plenty of advertisements for bird garden equipment and various bird foods.

It is of course quite possible to attract birds to the garden without the need for such elaborate devices. One can simply throw kitchen scraps onto the lawn, and these will usually be devoured eagerly by many species, especially in cold weather. But this can make for an untidy garden, and also sometimes attract the attention of small mammals such as squirrels and even rats, as well as exposing the feeding birds to danger from predators such as hunting cats.

For many reasons it is far better to provide food where the birds can feed in relative peace – such as on a bird table or from special bird feeders.

Bird tables

Many types of bird table are available, but sometimes it is best to choose a relatively simple design. Tables with complicated designs, such as thatched roofs, may look interesting, but they can be very awkward to clean, and many birds are wary of feeding underneath a low roof, preferring an uninterrupted view of the sky and surroundings.

Some bird tables incorporate a nest box into the roof, but this is quite unnecessary: it is unlikely any bird will take up residence so close to a table stocked with food and busy with other birds.

A simple tray attached to a pole can be perfectly good as a basic bird table (see photo on page 24), and it is not difficult to make your own. Most bird tables are pole-mounted, but it is also possible to hang the table from a branch or attach it to a window ledge.

If you decide to buy or make a roofed table, make sure that the roof overlaps the table so the rain does not get in. The table should have a rim to retain the food, but also gaps to allow water to drain away and to facilitate cleaning.

Bird feeders

Hanging feeders are of two basic types: those made of metal mesh, and those made from transparent plastic. The mesh types of feeder are suitable for large nuts such as peanuts and large sunflower seeds, while the tubular clear plastic feeders are primarily for finer seed, such as sunflower seeds or mixed seeds. The plastic tubes have feeding holes with landing perches, sometimes at more than one level. Home-made versions can be constructed from plastic drink bottles.

Peanuts are commonly offered in mesh webbing feeders, which are attractive to many birds – notably siskins. However, these feeders need monitoring carefully as birds can sometimes become entangled in them.

Accessories for use with hanging feeders include poles and hooks, and trays which can be attached at the feeder base to collect dropped seed. Some metal mesh feeders are formed into small cages or baskets, inside which you can place fat-based mixtures such as bird cakes or fat balls.

All feeders should be checked regularly to make sure that uneaten or rotten seed does not accumulate, and should be cleaned if necessary.

Home-made feeders

Hollow containers, such as half coconut shells, can be filled with a mixture of suet and seeds and then suspended from the bird table or branch. These will make good feeders for tits,

Key features of a bird table

An effective bird table should be:

- easy to reach
- safe for the birds
- simple to clean
- either free-draining or protected from the rain.

28

This plastic tube feeder provides a choice of access points, each with a convenient perch.

This pole-mounted feeder includes a tray for extra or fallen food – note the drainage holes.

A low-level table will attract species such as dunnock and song thrush which usually feed at or near the ground – but you need to make sure it is safe from attack by cats.

sparrows and greenfinches.

Treecreepers, nuthatches and woodpeckers will often feed from suet smeared into the ridges on the trunk of a tree, or into the crevices of a log. The latter can be tied above the ground to give the birds a safe feeding site.

Excluders

Squirrels can be a particular nuisance around bird tables. They are remarkably agile and acrobatic in their persistent efforts to reach food, including that in suspended feeders.

A number of products can be bought to solve this problem. One of the most effective of

these is a metal hanging feeder surrounded by a bell-shaped outer steel frame, the latter with holes too small to allow the squirrels access, but large enough for most seed-eating songbirds (see illustration on page 76). Another anti-squirrel device is a hanging feeder with a battery-powered feeding ring at the base, which is activated by the weight of a squirrel and flips round, unnerving and dislodging the squirrel. Squirrels soon learn to avoid this feeder and leave it strictly for the birds.

Yet another excluding device is an open tray with an adjustable dome above, the height of which can be varied to exclude larger birds such as collared doves. This can be suspended or mounted on a pole. A simple method of excluding squirrels is to suspend feeders from a wire (or clothes line) that is out of reach of even the most athletic of squirrels.

When to feed

In cold winter weather birds benefit greatly from feeding, as their energy is depleted through increased loss of body heat at this time of the year. This affects the smaller species more than larger birds, as the ratio of their surface area to body mass is so much greater.

However, shortages of food can occur at almost any season, such as after periods of prolonged rain, or as a consequence of failures in caterpillar emergence due to earlier bad weather affecting the adult insects at egg-laying time. Such shortages are hard to predict or assess, so the current advice is that we should feed our garden birds all year round, even though there will be periods when some species will be concentrating mainly on abundant natural supplies.

There will nearly always be birds around the garden that will take advantage of food offered at any season.

In summer the lawn becomes a feeding ground and dense bushes offer safe nesting sites.

Spring and summer
During the spring and early summer, offer highly nutritious (high-protein) foods such as insectivore mixes, sunflower seeds, oatmeal, vine fruits (currants, raisins, sultanas), mealworms or grated cheese.

Not recommended are bread, fat or loose peanuts. Whole peanuts can choke nestlings (although peanut granules are acceptable), while dry bread can swell inside the stomach. Peanut feeders are fine as long as the birds cannot remove the nuts whole. Ideally, make fresh water available also.

Protein-rich foods with dried insects incorporated are especially welcome. Black sunflower seeds, oatmeal and grated cheese are good, as are mealworms, and fruits such as apples, pears, and even bananas and grapes. Soaked cat and dog food is also good, but make sure it is well out of reach of rats.

At this time the birds need to build up their energies for the breeding season, and they and their offspring will benefit from high-calorie extra food. Many garden birds feed their hungry nestlings on high-energy insects (either adults or larvae such as caterpillars), but the food we put out will help keep the adults fit and healthy during this stressful time.

Towards late summer and early autumn, the amount of food offered can be reduced. There are usually plenty of natural sources of food available at this time, and the parents are no longer involved in the energetic business of feeding their young.

Autumn and winter
In late autumn and winter, food is extremely important for all garden birds, as natural supplies, especially of insects, are now much diminished. Foods with a high fat content will help give them extra energy. Regular feeding with high-energy sunflower kernels, peanuts and peanut granules, dried fruits and fat-rich foods is now the order of the day. Sunflower seeds may attract nuthatches as well as greenfinches and other commoner species.

When snow and ice cover the ground in winter, birds are really up against it. At this time extra feeding can be a life-saver, while evergreens provide welcome cover.

If you have fruit trees in your garden, some of the ripe fruit should be left under the trees for thrushes, blackbirds and starlings. It is best to put food out early, and twice a day (or more) during very cold weather. If the food disappears quickly, then put out more, but always try to adjust the supply so that surplus food is not left lying around.

Remember that even in the winter birds will drink and sometimes bathe, so don't forget to top up the bird bath.

Hygiene

With large quantities of food in the garden, the matter of hygiene becomes important. Always try to adjust the quantities offered to the demand, and remove any uneaten food as often as possible.

In spring and summer it is particularly important to pay attention to hygiene, as in warm weather food can quickly become unpalatable and even dangerous. Pay special attention to the state of bird tables and low-turnover peanut feeders. If they seem to be mouldy, serious cleaning is indicated. Brush and clean the bird table surface regularly to remove droppings and mouldy scraps of food, using a weak disinfectant solution.

Keep an eye also on the water in birdbaths, and clean these from time to time as well, changing the water every day in warm weather. Make sure you rinse the surfaces very thoroughly after disinfecting, to remove all traces of chemical cleaner.

It is also advisable to clean all the bird feeders and other apparatus outside the house, using a separate set of brushes and cloths; always remember to wash your hands thoroughly afterwards.

Top ten tips

The **BTO's Garden BirdWatch** scheme has issued a useful set of top ten tips for feeding garden birds:

1 Only put out as much food as can be consumed in a day or two. Never allow food or detritus to accumulate. Reduce food at quiet times.

2 Keep feeders reasonably clean and move them around the garden periodically to prevent infectious droppings from building up in one place.

3 In the nesting season avoid using whole peanuts. Either chop them up or provide them in a mesh peanut feeder from which adult birds can only take small fragments.

4 Try to have reasonably clean water available at all times for bathing as well as drinking – never add salt or chemicals.

5 Don't put out salty snacks, highly flavoured foods, uncooked rice, whole bacon rinds or unsoaked desiccated coconut, which can be fatal to birds.

6 Keep food away from cover in which a cat could hide. Consider using electronic cat scarers – these should be moved regularly.

7 But if sparrowhawks are present, place feeders next to shrubs to allow birds to escape. Clip the shrubs back hard at the base so cats cannot hide.

8 Provide a wide variety of different foods in different positions and types of feeder.

9 Cereal grain such as wheat attracts pigeons. Use better-quality pure foods such as black sunflower seeds or peanuts.

10 Stick to natural foods, rather than chemically altered or processed foods such as margarine.

Gardens for nesting birds

In addition to being a re-fuelling station for wild birds, your garden can also provide them with nesting opportunities. Indeed, gardens provide a network of green spaces that supports a huge population of breeding birds, some of which have become rather less common in the open countryside. In fact, when added together, gardens cover a larger area than nature reserves.

Of course, not all our native songbirds are suited to breeding in gardens – skylarks, for instance, need open fields and broad horizons, and nightingales are restricted mainly to woodland, heath or marshy areas with a rich scrubby undergrowth. But many birds of woodland, hedgerow and mixed farmland are also at home in gardens. Robins, wrens, blackbirds and chaffinches are some of the commonest garden birds, but their original habitat was mainly woodland, scrub or heath. Some species which probably nested originally on cliffs – for example, swifts, house martins and jackdaws – are nowadays equally at home nesting on houses, and feeding in or around the garden.

There are a number of advantages for birds that choose to nest in gardens. Gardens tend to be more varied than natural sites – or at least they contain many different habitats within a relatively small area. Wildlife-friendly gardens offer a range of potential 'natural' nest sites, including mature trees, dense bushes and hedges, and also the protective cover of climbing plants. Gardens also usually provide birds with a more reliable source of food than wild sites, especially if extra feeding is provided.

Nest boxes

Over 60 species of birds are recorded as having used nest boxes, although some take to them more readily than others. Small songbirds such as blue and great tits, and more rarely coal tits, which naturally nest in holes in trees, switch gratefully

A well-positioned nest box may well prove irresistible to prospecting birds in the early spring.

to nest boxes with a hole on one side.

The list of regular box nesters is quite long and includes house (and tree) sparrows, starlings, robins, spotted flycatchers, nuthatches, even house martins, tawny and barn owls and kestrels.

Tawny owls can sometimes be persuaded to use open-topped 'chimney' nest boxes. If you have these owls around your garden, and you have a suitable tree, it might be worth mounting such a box, at a slight angle, at least 3 m (10 ft) high, making it look as much like a natural hole as possible.

Special barn owl boxes are also available and can be successful if they are carefully sited close to known barn owl habitats.

Most boxes are made from wood, and these are available in a wide range of designs, aimed at different target species. The diameter of the entrance hole is important as it will have a bearing on which species can use the box:

- 25 mm (1 in) for blue tits or coal tits
- 28 mm (1.1 in) for great tits or tree sparrows
- 32 mm (1.25 in) for house sparrows or nuthatches
- 45 mm (1.75 in) for starlings
- 50 mm (2 in) for great spotted woodpeckers.

In addition to boxes with a small hole in one side, there are open, ledge-style boxes which suit robins and wrens, and also

Three different types of nest box

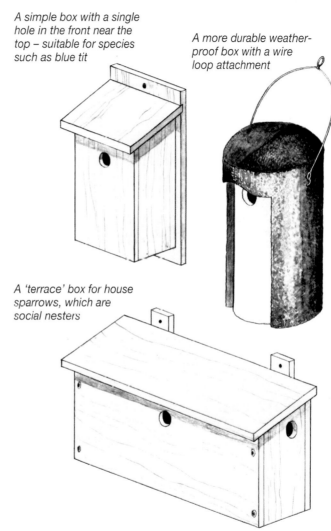

A simple box with a single hole in the front near the top – suitable for species such as blue tit

A more durable weatherproof box with a wire loop attachment

A 'terrace' box for house sparrows, which are social nesters

large boxes with more than one entrance to encourage house sparrows, which like to nest close together.

Woven boxes are also useful, and these may be used as over-

night roosting sites as well as for nesting. Special containers filled with wool provide nesting materials, and may further encourage birds to take up residence in the garden. More

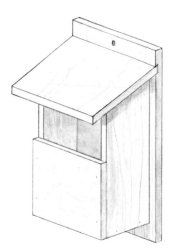

An open-fronted box – ideal for robins or, if you are lucky, a pair of spotted flycatchers

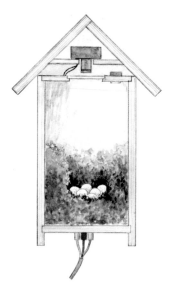

A section through a nest box with a roof-mounted camera, allowing live monitoring of nesting activities

 Installing cameras

Special nestboxes (and sometimes bird tables) are now available equipped with tiny cameras, which allow monitoring of the birds' activities without distur-bance. The typical box has a tiny camera and microphone mounted in the roof, and low-level lighting which does not disturb the birds.

Live pictures can be transmitted to a TV, video or computer, allowing you to eaves-drop on the birds and watch nest-building, egg-laying, and the hatching and feeding of the brood. It is fascinating to observe wild birds feeding at close quarters or bringing food in to their nestlings. If you have time and patience, you can even add to our knowledge by recording what types of food are brought to the nest, and with what frequency.

durable are nest boxes made from a combination of concrete and sawdust. These withstand the weather much better than wood and are virtually inde-structible (see picture on previous page).

Position and timing

When positioning a nest box, always fix it firmly to a wall, post or tree trunk, out of reach of danger but within easy reach for regular cleaning (outside the breeding season). It also helps if there is a direct flight-path to the entrance. Shelter from the wind, rain and direct sun is also desirable, so if possible ensure that the box faces somewhere between north-east and south-east.

The best time of year to put up nest boxes is after the breeding season is over – i.e. in the autumn – and ideally before November. This gives the local birds plenty of time to get used to them before the following breeding season starts at the turn of the year and in the early spring. The box can be 'baited' with a little moss. This will encourage winter-roosting birds to use it, and will also increase the chances of the box being used for nesting in the following spring.

Do not be discouraged if a box is ignored for the first year, or even longer – although nest boxes are sometimes used immediately. Even if a box seems to be ignored, birds may actually be using it as a safe roosting site.

Two ways of deterring unwanted visitors to a nest box

A plastic or metal tube extends and protects the entrance hole.

A metal plate stops the hole diameter from becoming enlarged.

Nesting habits

Birds vary widely in their preferred nesting habits (see table on page 39). Some, like rooks and herons, and to a lesser degree house sparrows, are colonial birds, nearly always nesting close to others of their species. However, most of our garden birds nest as isolated pairs, often defending their territories energetically.

Several species, including great tits, blackbirds, thrushes and robins, establish their breeding territories as soon as the days begin to lengthen in winter – and as spring draws near, the level and complexity of bird song, especially at dawn, is evidence of the energy birds devote to their breeding cycles.

Now is the time to watch as the birds inspect possible nesting sites. You may notice a blackbird spending time prospecting in a particular shrub, or a great tit visiting a nest box to see if it is suitable. If you have a barn or stables, these may well attract the attention of a passing swallow, and if you are lucky, house martins will start to build their neat mud nests under the eaves of the house.

Old trees should be retained as far as possible, especially if, like this hollow ash, they have natural holes and crevices which provide ample nesting opportunities.

Nesting sites

The table opposite shows the usual nesting sites for the commonest birds. They also indicate where a particular species uses a nest box, and if so whether regularly or more rarely. Those birds which are commonest in gardens are marked with an asterisk.

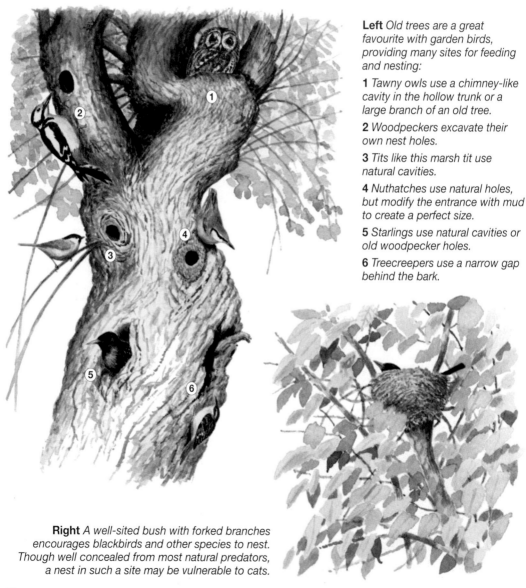

Left *Old trees are a great favourite with garden birds, providing many sites for feeding and nesting:*

1 *Tawny owls use a chimney-like cavity in the hollow trunk or a large branch of an old tree.*

2 *Woodpeckers excavate their own nest holes.*

3 *Tits like this marsh tit use natural cavities.*

4 *Nuthatches use natural holes, but modify the entrance with mud to create a perfect size.*

5 *Starlings use natural cavities or old woodpecker holes.*

6 *Treecreepers use a narrow gap behind the bark.*

Right *A well-sited bush with forked branches encourages blackbirds and other species to nest. Though well concealed from most natural predators, a nest in such a site may be vulnerable to cats.*

Nesting sites of birds

Key

B	commonly uses box
(B)	uses box more rarely
C	colonial
H	hole nester,

Birds that nest in trees

grey heron **C**	*see page* 41
sparrowhawk	42
kestrel **H(B)**	43
stock dove **H**	44
woodpigeon*	45
collared dove*	45
turtle dove	46
ring-necked parakeet **H**	46
barn owl **H**	47
tawny owl **H**	48
green woodpecker **H**	48
great spotted woodpecker **H**	49
lesser spotted woodpecker **H**	49
fieldfare	55
redwing	56
mistle thrush	57
goldcrest*	60
marsh tit **H**	62
coal tit **H**	62
blue tit* **HB**	63
great tit* **HB**	63
nuthatch **H**	64

treecreeper	64
jay	65
magpie*	65
rook **C**	66
carrion/hooded crow	67
starling* **H**	67
chaffinch*	69
siskin	71
linnet	72
common redpoll	72
yellowhammer	72

Birds that nest on or close to the ground

mallard	*see page* 42
pheasant	43
yellow wagtail	52
willow warbler	59

Birds that nest in hedges or bushes

wren*	*see page* 53
dunnock*	53
robin* **B**	54
fieldfare	55
blackbird*	55
song thrush*	56
redwing	56
whitethroat	57
lesser whitethroat	58
garden warbler	58

blackcap*	59
chiffchaff	59
spotted flycatcher **(B)**	60
long-tailed tit*	61
chaffinch*	69
bullfinch	70
greenfinch*	70
goldfinch*	72
linnet	72
common redpoll	72
yellowhammer	72

Birds that nest on houses

feral pigeon*	*see page* 45
swift* **H(B)**	50
swallow* **(B)**	50
house martin* **(B)**	50
pied wagtail*	52
jackdaw* **H**	66
starling* **H**	67
house sparrow* **B(C)**	68

Birds that nest on or near water

moorhen	*see page* 43
black-headed gull	44
common gull	44
kingfisher **H** (bank)	48
grey wagtail	51
reed bunting	73

Kestrels usually nest in hollow trees, but will occasionally use large, specially designed nest boxes. They feed mainly on small rodents.

Directory of garden birds

This directory gives short descriptions of the birds you're most likely to see in your garden. Some of them are unlikely to be absent from any garden – blackbird, wren, chaffinch or woodpigeon, for instance – while others, such as turtle dove, kingfisher or lesser spotted woodpecker, are much rarer visitors to most gardens.

Of course gardens vary enormously in shape, size, soil and location, and a garden next to open country will attract a somewhat different set of birds from a tiny patch behind a city terrace. Yet very few gardens are completely without birds.

Birds are also unpredictable, and many unusual species may put in an appearance in the garden from time to time, especially if you provide a variety of cover, and offer a suitable range of food. The hints provided elsewhere in this book will help you to increase the number and variety of birds

Birds by season: winter visitors

Bird species that are only likely to be seen in gardens in the winter

fieldfare	*see page* 55
gull	
black-headed*	44
common	44
redwing*	56
siskin	71
waxwing	53

Birds by season: resident species
Birds that can be seen in gardens throughout the year

blackbird*	*see page* 55	pigeon	
bullfinch	70	feral*	45
bunting, reed	73	wood-*	45
chaffinch*	69	redpoll, common	72
crow, carrion/hooded	67	robin*	54
dove		rook	66
collared*	45	sparrow, house*	68
stock	44	sparrowhawk	42
dunnock*	53	starling*	67
goldcrest	60	thrush	
goldfinch*	72	mistle	57
greenfinch*	70	song*	56
heron, grey	41	tit	
jackdaw*	66	blue*	63
jay	65	coal	62
kestrel	43	great*	63
kingfisher	48	long-tailed*	61
linnet	72	marsh	62
magpie*	65	treecreeper	64
mallard	42	wagtail	
moorhen	43	grey	51
nuthatch	64	pied*	52
owl		woodpecker	
barn	47	great spotted	49
tawny	48	green	48
parakeet, ring-necked	46	lesser spotted	49
pheasant	43	wren*	53
		yellowhammer	72

Birds by season: summer visitors

Bird species that are only likely to be seen in gardens in the summer

blackcap*	*see page* 59
(overwinters increasingly)	
chiffchaff	59
cuckoo	46
dove, turtle	46
flycatcher, spotted	60
martin, house*	50
swallow*	50
swift*	50
wagtail, yellow	52
warbler	
garden	58
willow	59
whitethroat	57
lesser	58

An aristocrat amongst wetland birds, the stately grey heron is an occasional visitor to garden ponds.

coming into your garden, whatever type of garden you have.

The entries in this directory are in systematic sequence so that related species are close together, thus aiding comparisons. The commonest garden birds are highlighted with an asterisk (*) and each species is labelled either **R** (resident species), **S** (summer visitor) or **W** (winter visitor).

The special panels in this section highlight comparisons between potentially confusing species, with notes to aid identification.

Grey heron R
Ardea cinerea
This very large waterbird is instantly recognisable from its long neck and legs, and its slow, ponderous flight, during which the neck is pulled in close to the body, with the legs trailing behind.

Herons stand still for long periods at the water's edge when hunting, mainly for fish or frogs. They are communal breeders, using traditional heronries, which may have up to 200 nests, though most have up to about 40 pairs. They nest and lay early in the season,

before most of the trees have come into leaf.

Herons often visit gardens with a large pond, lake or other water feature, especially if there are fish to be caught. Although herons may fly long distances to feed, gardens close to wetland sites or a heronry will usually be visited more often. Shy birds, herons often fly into the garden early in the morning. They may be encouraged by wildlife-rich ponds, but can be a nuisance if you stock valuable fish.

Distribution and status
In recent years heron numbers have increased steadily, perhaps as a result of a series of mild winters. In very cold weather

Bird remains and piles of feathers are usually a sign that a sparrowhawk is about, but they do not reduce the numbers of our garden songbirds.

they find it hard to get enough food, and many perish.

Habitat preference
Wetlands, including ponds, rivers and lakes, but also coastal sites, especially rocky shores, such as in the west of Scotland or Ireland.

Food preference
Fish, frogs, sometimes small mammals and birds.

Mallard R
Anas platyrhynchos
This medium-sized duck is a familiar sight near water in parks and gardens, and in the wild. The female is a dull streaked brown, and the male in breeding plumage has a bright-green head.

Although mallards are not usually attracted to small gardens, if you have a large area with a sizeable pond or stream,

they may turn up sooner or later. They sometimes nest quite a distance from water, and the mother will usually try to lead her ducklings to the relative safety of water soon after they hatch.

Mallards take a wide range of food, including invertebrates as well as waterweeds. They are also very fond of snails, and will help rid the garden of molluscs, even gulping down the largest of garden snails.

Distribution and status
Common throughout Britain.

Habitat preference
Lakes, ponds, rivers, streams; also waterside meadows, pastures, parks and large gardens.

Food preference
Aquatic animals and plants; aquatic and terrestrial snails, worms.

Sparrowhawk R
Accipiter nisus
These agile, broad-winged hunters, and specialist bird-killers, are increasingly being seen in gardens as well as in wooded countryside.

Many people worry that sparrowhawks are a cause of recent declines in songbird populations, but there is no evidence to support this. Rather, their increase is evidence of a healthier environment with plenty of prey species in urban areas. Female sparrowhawks, which are considerably larger than males, tend to take bigger prey such as collared doves (of which there are plenty), while the males tackle smaller species such as great tits and blackbirds.

Distribution and status
Mainly a woodland bird, but often found in parks and gardens as well. In more natural sites they use trees and hedges as a screen while hunting, but terraced houses offer equally good cover.

Habitat preference
Mixed habitat with belts of trees, and adjacent open areas for hunting.

Food preference
Small to medium-sized birds.

Kestrel R
Falco tinnunculus
One of our commonest birds of prey, perhaps most often seen hovering over rough grassland (often at the roadside) as it scans the ground below for prey. This usually consists of small mammals such as voles or mice, but it may also take small birds or even earthworms.

Kestrels are rather less frequent in gardens than sparrowhawks, but will sometimes nest in an old tree (see page 39), especially if there is grassland nearby, occasionally making use of a large nest box.

Distribution and status
Common throughout, but has declined in recent years, especially in western England, probably due to loss of habitat, such as the removal of hedgerows.

Habitat preference
Needs open grassland, heath or moorland over which to hunt. Also found in cities, nesting on tall buildings such as church spires or office blocks.

Food preference
Mainly small mammals, small birds, worms, insects.

Pheasant R
Phasianus colchicus
Britain's most numerous game bird, native to Central Asia and probably introduced by the Normans, or maybe even the Romans. Populations are now kept up artificially by breeding and feeding, mainly for the 'sport' of shooting. The male seen at close quarters is beautiful, with shiny, colourful plumage and long tail streamers; the female is a drab grey-brown. One cock bird mates with several females.

Gardens close to open country sometimes attract pheasants, especially if grain and similar scraps are available on the ground, and the birds may approach close to houses when particularly hungry in cold weather.

Distribution and status
Throughout, but commonest in southern England, north to Yorkshire.

Habitat preference
Wooded agricultural land, with shrubs and adjacent fields. Increasingly attracted to gardens to feed, where they can be quite tame.

Food preference
Grain, shoots, insects (eaten mainly by young birds).

Moorhen R
Gallinula chloropus
Note the blackish plumage, with white tail flashes, and the bright red bill, tipped yellow. Moorhens have very long toes, and although their feet are not webbed they can swim well. They build a floating nest, and though nearly always found near water, they feed mainly on land, especially on damp grassland.

Distribution and status
Widespread and common, especially in lowland sites near water.

A large garden pond with fringing vegetation may attract a moorhen to build its semi-floating nest.

Habitat preference
Usually rather secretive and shy, moorhens can be rather common around ponds, lakes and rivers, and in other damp habitats close to water. Not usually seen in the garden unless you have a large pond or lake, with some cover such as reeds at the margins.

Food preference
Small invertebrates, water weeds, seeds.

Black-headed gull* R/W
Larus ridibundus
Our commonest small gull, with agile flight, and a chocolate-brown head in summer, though in winter the head has just a few small dark spots. The narrow wings have a bright white flash along the leading edge. This gull often moves inland in winter to feed, for example, on ploughed land or playing fields and neighbouring gardens.

Distribution and status
Widespread, both at the coast and inland. Mainly a winter visitor to gardens.

Habitat preference
In winter and during hard weather these gulls sometimes visit gardens for scraps of food, usually in small flocks, or probe for worms and grubs on lawns, parks and fields.

Food preference
Omnivorous: small animals, seeds, and scraps of all kinds.

Common gull R/W
Larus canus
Somewhat larger and stockier than the black-headed gull, with black wingtips and white 'mirrors'. The back and upper wings are dove grey. Note also the absence of the white flash at the leading edge of the wing, which is slightly broader than that of the black-headed gull.

Distribution and status
Not as common as black-headed gulls, breeding mainly in northern Britain and Ireland. In winter they are often seen with black-headed gulls, sometimes in mixed flocks.

Habitat preference
They occasionally visit gardens during hard weather, or probe for worms and grubs on lawns, parks and playing fields, often in the company of black-headed gulls.

Food preference
Omnivorous: small animals, seeds, and scraps of all kinds.

Stock dove R
Columba oenas
Smaller than the woodpigeon, and rather uniformly grey, with few distinctive markings except a short, dark double wingbar. The call is a soft two-syllable cooing.

Distribution and status
Quite common, but often overlooked.

Habitat preference
Likes open country, especially wooded farmland, but may be seen around gardens, especially if there are old trees with nesting holes. Not often seen feeding in the open, however.

Food preference
Mainly seeds.

Woodpigeons are now regular visitors to parks and gardens, often finding their food from the ground.

Collared doves now among our commonest garden birds. They are very fond of grain and will readily feed at bird tables.

Woodpigeon* R
Columba palumbus
Our largest pigeon – very bulky and rather ungainly on the ground. There is a white patch on the neck, and the white wing patches are very obvious in flight. Woodpigeons often gather in huge flocks over open country. The call is a pleasant long cooing with many syllables, ending abruptly.

Woodpigeons can sometimes be a nuisance in the garden, feeding on vegetable crops. They look somewhat ungainly as they waddle about the lawn in search of scraps or seeds dropped from feeders.

Distribution and status
Very common.

Habitat preference
Found in a wide range of habitats, from open fields to woodland and parks – but also increasingly in gardens, where they are attracted to food, especially grain.

Food preference
Seeds, berries, shoots; also scraps.

Feral pigeon* R
Columba livia
This is the common small 'pigeon' found in most cities and towns. Descended from the wild rock dove, this semi-domesticated form comes in a wide range of colours and patterns, although most birds retain the white rump of the ancestral form.

Distribution and status
Common, especially in urban areas.

Habitat preference
Towns and cities, parks and gardens, but also in open countryside, and on sea-cliffs, where they sometimes inter-breed with pure wild rock doves.

Food preference
Seeds, and scraps of all sorts.

Collared dove* R
Streptopelia decaocto
A small dove with pale grey-beige plumage, and with an incomplete black, white-edged collar (though the white edge is not very conspicuous). The tail has a white tip that is most noticeable in flight.

The song is a very characteristic cooing, of three syllables, accented on the second. This can sound cuckoo-like if half-heard, or incomplete, and may explain some unexpected cuckoo records.

Distribution and status
First recorded in Britain in the early 1950s, the collared dove is now common everywhere in the country, especially in towns, villages and suburban areas. This is one of the most remarkable and rapid colonisations by any bird, collared doves having spread steadily north and west throughout Europe from Turkey and nearby regions over the last half-century.

Habitat preference
Thrives best near human habitations, and can often be seen in gardens, where it regularly visits bird tables. Nowadays one of our commonest garden birds.

Food preference
Mainly seeds, especially grain.

45

Turtle dove S
Streptopelia turtur
A small, dainty dove with warm chestnut plumage and white outer tail feathers. The outline is slender, and the tail rather long. Turtle doves arrive in late April or May, and return to their African wintering grounds in September. The song is a very distinctive soft, purring call, which carries quite a distance, but which is rather quiet and difficult to locate. Turtle doves are shy birds, often clinging to cover, so that they can be very hard to spot.

Distribution and status
Formerly much commoner, turtle doves have suffered a steep decline in recent years, probably because of droughts in Africa combined with agricultural 'improvements' in Britain. Found mainly in the south and east.

Habitat preference
Mainly in wooded country and heathland, but sometimes seen in or near gardens, especially around large, quiet parks or near open country.

Food preference
Mainly seeds.

Ring-necked (rose-ringed) parakeet R
Psittacula krameri
This exotic parrot is native to Asia. It is a bright, vivid green, with a long tail and a bright-red bill, and is quite unlike any other garden bird. Like many parrots, it is sociable and has a loud, screeching call. Colonies breed mainly in tree holes.

Distribution and status
Only established in certain places, especially in parts of suburban London – for example, in the south-east and south-west of the city.

Habitat preference
Parkland and gardens with tall trees nearby. They roost in noisy colonies, and sometimes visit gardens, taking peanuts and the like from bird tables and feeders.

Food preference
Fruit, seeds, berries; also scraps.

Cuckoo S
Cuculus canorus
Well-known from the call of the male bird, cuckoos are rather secretive and can be hard to locate. They look rather like small birds of prey as they glide and flutter with their long, pointed wings, long tail and barred plumage. The female utters a strange bubbling call.

Often active and noisy at night, tawny owls roost quietly by day hidden close to the trunk, as here in an ivy-clad tree.

often appears white at night – which may even be responsible for some reports of ghosts, especially in churchyards.

Barn owls are most often seen flying low over the ground at dusk or dawn, searching for small mammals. The flight is very buoyant and totally silent as the owl homes in on its prey, partly with the help of its highly sensitive hearing. Sounds are focused on the ears by the facial discs, which act rather like satellite dishes to concentrate the sound waves.

Distribution and status
Rather uncommon except in lowland farmland with rough grassland, though in the fenlands of eastern England these beautiful owls are still a familiar sight.

Habitat preference
The ideal habitat is a mixture of rough grassland, heath and marshy areas, with old trees or abandoned farm buildings for nesting. Barn owls are not very often seen in gardens, but they can be persuaded to nest in special large boxes if these are suitably positioned.

Food preference
Mainly voles, mice, rats and shrews.

Cuckoos are brood parasites of small songbirds, including dunnock, meadow pipit and reed warbler. The female cuckoo lays a single egg in the host's nest, and on hatching the young cuckoo then pushes the other eggs out of the nest, after which it receives all the food brought by the parent hosts. It seems that different individual cuckoos specialise in parasitising different host species, and lay eggs which match the pattern and size of those of the parasitised species. Recent research has shown that the young cuckoo chick even mimics the call of the hungry young nestlings of the host, thus helping to fool the foster parents.

Distribution and status
Found throughout, though it has suffered a marked decline in recent years.

Habitat preference
Found in a wide range of habitats, including woodland, heath, moorland and reedbeds. Sometimes seen in larger gardens.

Food preference
Mainly caterpillars, including the distasteful hairy caterpillars avoided by most other birds.

Barn owl R
Tyto alba
Only two of our owls are likely to be seen (or heard) in gardens: the barn owl and the tawny owl. The barn owl is medium-sized with very pale plumage that

If you have a pond or stream you may be lucky enough to spot a kingfisher.

Kingfisher R
Alcedo atthis

One of our most attractive and exciting birds thanks to its shiny bright colours – metallic blues and greens, and a rich orange underside. The kingfisher is usually first seen when it is flushed from a riverbank, and flies low and straight over the water surface, often uttering a sharp, high-pitched piping whistle.

Distribution and status
Most common in lowland and central England. Populations tend to crash in severe winters, when many birds die.

Habitat preference
Kingfishers prefer slow-moving or still waters, such as rivers, canals, reservoirs, lakes and ponds. They can sometimes be seen on garden lakes and ponds, especially if small fish are available.

Food preference
Small fish, and aquatic invertebrates such as insect larvae.

Green woodpecker R
Picus viridis

This chunky, rather wild-eyed woodland bird is often seen in gardens close to trees or heathland, especially if there are large lawns. Green wood-peckers like nothing better than to grub for ants, and lawns are ideal for this, especially on light, sandy soils.

The bright-green plumage and yellow rump (obvious in flight) make a splendid sight. The flight is bounding and somewhat heavy. The loud, laughing 'yaffle' call is highly characteristic and carries a long distance.

Distribution and status
Widespread, but commonest in southern England.

Habitat preference
Woodland, especially in the neighbourhood of open meadows or heath. Increasingly seen in

Tawny owl R
Strix aluco

Our commonest owl, often detected by its calls – the familiar drawn-out, tremulous hoot and a sharp 'kee-wick'. The brown, dappled, camou-flaged plumage (see page 46), combined with its strictly nocturnal habits, make it very hard to spot. Tawny owls feed on small mammals, but also sometimes take roosting birds, and even earth-worms from lawns.

Distribution and status
Widespread, but often overlooked. More often heard than seen, especially in late autumn when they are establishing their territories. Tawny owls will sometimes make use of large nest boxes.

Habitat preference
Prefers mixed woodland, but also found in wooded gardens and parks.

Food preference
Small mammals, small birds, worms.

gardens. Green woodpeckers require old trees for nesting (they excavate a hole, usually in oak or ash), combined with open ground for feeding.

Food preference
Ants, grubs.

Great spotted woodpecker R
Dendrocopos major
Our commonest woodpecker – thrush-sized, with black-and-white plumage and red under the base of the tail. The large white patches on the back are distinctive. The flight is undulating. This is the woodpecker responsible for the loud drumming on a hollow tree that is heard during the breeding season.

Distribution and status
Widespread, with a steady increase since the 1970s.

Habitat preference
Woodland, copses and parkland. Also increasingly in gardens, where they sometimes visit feeding stations.

Food preference
Insects, especially those in wood or bark. Fat and other foods from bird tables (mainly in winter).

Lesser spotted woodpecker R
Dendrocopos minor
Our smallest woodpecker, only about the size of a sparrow, and easily overlooked. The back has horizontal white bands, and the male has a red cap. The call is high-pitched and nasal. This species sometimes drums, but more softly than the great spotted woodpecker.

Distribution and status
The numbers of lesser spotted woodpeckers have declined steeply since the early 1980s, perhaps due to the loss of elm trees killed by Dutch elm disease, plus a general 'cleaning up' of the countryside by the removal of hedges and older trees.

Habitat preference
Mixed woods, riverside trees such as willows and poplars; also parks and sometimes gardens.

Food preference
Insects, especially those in wood or bark.

Great spotted woodpeckers excavate their nest holes in the trunk of tree. They are becoming more frequent garden visitors.

Swift* S
Apus apus
The swift is a fast-flying bird with blackish-brown plumage and a pale chin (though this is not usually obvious), long, sickle-shaped wings and a shallowly forked tail.

Swifts spend most of their life on the wing, often for weeks at a stretch outside the breeding season – even apparently napping whilst airborne! In fact, if a swift is grounded (for example, after a rainstorm) it may be doomed, as it finds it difficult to take off from a horizontal surface. Screaming parties of several birds display in the summer, sometimes circling to a great height in the evenings.

Distribution and status
Swifts are commonest in central, southern and eastern England. They arrive later than swallows and martins (usually in early May), and also leave earlier (from mid-August).

Habitat preference
Swifts breed naturally in crevices in cliffs, but nowadays prefer the eaves of houses, church towers and similar man-made sites.

Though not strictly speaking garden birds, they are a common sight in the airspace over gardens, and find the roofs of older terraced houses to their liking for nesting. Specialist swift nest boxes are now available.

Food preference
Insects – always caught in flight.

Swallow* S
Hirundo rustica
A slim, elegant bird with a long tail and fine streamers; juveniles have shorter tails. Swallows are metallic blue above, with a red-brown chin and forehead. They often feed at low levels, hunting flying insects in smooth, flowing flight. Sometimes they can be seen flying low over water, dipping their beaks to sip from the surface of a pond.

Distribution and status
Common throughout, arriving in April.

Habitat preference
Swallows nest mainly in farm buildings, stables, sheds and the like, or under bridges. The nest is an open cup made of grasses and mud. Swallows tend to hunt above meadows and pastures, and also over ponds, lakes and rivers. Often seen around gardens, especially if there are outbuildings with access for nesting.

Food preference
Insects – mostly caught in flight.

House martin* S
Delichon urbica
Smaller and more compact than the swallow, with metallic blue-black plumage above and pure white below, and with an obvious white rump. The tail is much less deeply forked. The flight is a bit different too, being more fluttery, interspersed with glides. House martins usually hunt at a higher level than swallows.

Distribution and status
Common and widespread, arriving around mid to late April.

Swallows may be spotted swooping over the garden, or perhaps nesting in an open stable or shed.

Swallow, swift or martin?

Swallows, swifts and our two species of martin are often confused. But with practice they can usually be distinguished quite easily.

The **swift** is the largest, but the scale is difficult to judge as it often flies very high – though it may hunt low if the weather reduces the numbers of high-flying insects. Swifts are nearly always in groups, and have long, narrow wings and a short, notched tail. Their dark-brown plumage looks black from a distance, and they make shrill, screaming calls.

Swallows are graceful and swooping in flight, and are dark blue above and pale beneath. The adults have a forked tail, with two long, trailing streamers. They are most likely to be confused with house martins, but lack the white rump of the latter. However, young swallows don't have the long tail streamers and look more like house martins. Swallows are usually seen gliding low over meadows, or flying in and out of an outhouse, stable or shed to an open, cup-shaped mud nest.

House martins are slightly smaller than swallows and have a more fluttery flight. They are also more sociable, nesting and hunting in groups. Look out for the distinctive white rump. Their nests are oval mud structures with a small entrance at the top, and are usually built under the eaves.

Sand martins are not often seen in or around gardens. They are even smaller, with pale-brown plumage above, paler beneath, and a neckband. The tail is short and notched. They are colonial nesters, excavating holes in sandy banks.

Habitat preference

Usually nests on buildings, including under the eaves of houses, in small or large colonies. The nest is a sealed dome of mud with an entrance hole at the top. House martins may sometimes be attracted to a special artificial nest box.

Food preference

Insects – mostly caught in flight.

House martins create their domed nests using beakfuls of mud, usually under the eaves of a building.

Grey wagtail R
Motacilla cinerea

This large wagtail has a slaty-blue back, a long tail, and bright-yellow underparts and rump. It shows typical wagtail behaviour, with its rather bouncy flight, and almost constant flicking of the tail when on the ground. The call is a two-syllable 'tsee-sit'.

Distribution and status

A classic river bird of upland streams. Rather rarer in lowland eastern England.

Habitat preference

Almost always associated with water – typically along fast-flowing streams and shallow rivers, but also around gravel pits and reservoirs. This bird sometimes visits lakes and ponds, including those in

Pied wagtails are often seen on lawns. This one is collecting nesting material.

Distribution and status
Common throughout. Birds breeding in the north migrate south to overwinter in southern Britain.

Habitat preference
Found in most habitats except woodland, and often visits gardens.

Food preference
Small insects and other invertebrates, usually from the ground.

gardens, especially outside the breeding season.

Food preference
Insects and their larvae; occasionally small fish.

Pied wagtail* R/W
Motacilla alba
Our most familiar wagtail with its black-and-white plumage. It has a long, black tail with white outer tail feathers. The legs are also long and black. The flight call is a rather coarse double note: 'chiss-ick'.

Pied wagtails may often be seen feeding on garden lawns, from which they sometimes fly up to chase flying ants or other insects.

Yellow wagtail S
Motacilla flava
This dainty wagtail has a bright-yellow head, neck and underparts in the breeding season; the upper parts are olive green. The call is a distinctive high-pitched, rather thin 'tsee-ee'. Yellow wagtails are rather rare visitors to gardens, but may be seen if your garden adjoins open cropland or meadows.

Distribution and status
A summer visitor which has suffered a decline in recent years.

Habitat preference
Breeds mostly in crops or damp meadows – often associated with grazing livestock.

Rare and exotic-looking, waxwings sometimes arrive in flocks from Scandinavia, especially to north and east Britain. They are usually seen feeding on berries.

Food preference
Small insects and other invertebrates, usually taken from the ground.

Waxwing W
Bombycilla garrulus
This exotic-looking species has a crest, a yellow tip to its tail and red, wax-like markings on the wings from which it gets its name. It is about the size of a starling and looks rather dull brown when seen from a distance.

In certain years waxwings appear in surprisingly large numbers – usually in small groups and in unpredictable locations. They are fairly tame and approachable, and word tends to get around when waxwings are to be found in the area.

Distribution and status
Breeds in north-east Scandinavia and Russia. A regular autumn and winter visitor to Britain – normally scarce, but numbers vary from year to year.

Habitat preference
Attracted mainly to berry-bearing bushes and garden shrubs, such as guelder rose, cotoneaster and the like.

Food preference
Insects, seeds and berries. In winter they feed mainly on red berries.

Wren* R
Troglodytes troglodytes
The tiny, rotund wren is our smallest bird together with the goldcrest (and the firecrest). The short tail is often held cocked upright, and the flight is direct, with rapid wingbeats.

The song is a rich warble, with many trills – surprisingly loud for such a small bird. The alarm call is a robin-like 'teck-teck', which is sometimes slurred.

Wrens construct domed nests that are usually well hidden – for instance, in ivy or amongst the roots of a tree. However, they may sometimes nest in the corner of a little-used shed. Wrens can be rather secretive birds and are usually spotted as they flit at a low level from bush to bush.

Distribution and status
One of our commonest birds, but numbers decline after really hard winters. Individuals may huddle together for warmth on cold nights - over 60 have been found together in a single nest box.

Habitat preference
Found in most habitats, from dense woodland to heath, moorland, parks and gardens.

Food preference
Small insects, spiders and other invertebrates.

Dunnock* R
Prunella modularis
The dunnock is also known as a hedge sparrow, but this species is not a true sparrow. In shape it rather resembles a robin, with

This wren has typically built its nest hidden amongst the undergrowth.

Dunnocks tend to stick to the undergrowth, making forays to feed on the ground.

its thin bill. The head and breast are a slaty grey, the plumage otherwise brown and streaked.

Often overlooked in the garden, dunnocks tend to lurk in the foliage, making forays to feed in the open. They usually feed on the ground, often picking up fallen scraps, rather than on the bird table.

Dunnocks have a complex and fascinating sex life, some males mating with more than one female, some females with more than one male.

Distribution and status
Common and widespread, but easily overlooked.

Habitat preference
Woodland, parks and gardens.

Food preference
Mainly insects and seeds.

Robin* R
Erithacus rubecula

Probably our best-known garden bird, adorning many a Christmas card and catalogue. Both sexes have the distinctive orange-red breast, and their feisty behaviour makes them easy to spot.

The song, which is delivered in autumn as well as in spring, is a pleasantly clear, somewhat melancholy, descending series of rippling notes.

In the garden robins may become quite fearless and tame, sometimes following the gardener and picking insects from freshly dug soil.

Distribution and status
Common, with a slight increase in recent years.

Habitat preference
Mature deciduous woodland, but also found in hedgerows, parks and gardens.

Food preference
Mainly insects and seeds; sometimes fruit, especially in winter.

If you leave some fallen apples on the ground they will be welcomed by birds, including robins and blackbirds.

Hard winter frosts may force fieldfares into the garden, especially if there is fruit available.

Fieldfare W
Turdus pilaris
Slightly larger than a blackbird, this rather chunky thrush has quite bold markings, with chestnut back and wings, grey head and rump, and a black tail. The contrast between the dark tail, light grey rump and white underwings is very clear in flight, and flocks tend to make raw chattering calls – 'shak-shak-shak'.

Distribution and status
A regular winter visitor from Scandinavia.

Thrushes

Five species of thrush (genus *Turdus*) may be seen in the garden: blackbird, song thrush, mistle thrush, redwing and fieldfare.

The commonest by far is the **blackbird**, which is seen in almost all gardens. Both our resident thrushes – the **song thrush** and the **mistle thrush** – have become rarer, but are still regular garden visitors. These are brown with spotted undersides, but the mistle thrush is larger and much greyer.

Redwings and **fieldfares** are usually only seen in the winter, when they escape the colder weather in their Scandinavian breeding grounds. We see them in small parties, or even large flocks, and hard weather drives them into gardens to seek out tasty edible berries. Redwings show flashes of orange-red as they fly, but the fieldfare is the most colourful, with its chestnut back, grey head and rump, pale yellow underparts, speckled flanks and black tail. In size it is between the blackbird and the mistle thrush.

Habitat preference
Tends to be found in open country, such as ploughed fields, pasture, playing fields and the like – also in hedgerows (especially those with berries). In really cold weather, fieldfares will come into gardens, especially if there are berry-bearing trees and shrubs, or apple trees.

Food preference
Invertebrates in fields; fruits and berries in hedgerows and gardens.

Blackbird* R
Turdus merula
One of our commonest and most prominent garden birds, and instantly recognisable: the adult male is jet black with a yellow bill, the female brown, and young birds a rather russet

brown. Some individuals show white flecks.

The song of the blackbird is one of our finest – very clear, loud and tuneful. The alarm call is a metallic 'tsink-tsink' or a chatter.

Distribution and status
Very common throughout.

Habitat preference
Woodland, hedgerows, parkland and gardens

Food preference
Insects, worms; also seeds, fruits and scraps.

During the breeding season, with hungry nestlings to feed, birds such as this blackbird will benefit from extra feeding.

Song thrush* R
Turdus philomelos
This small thrush has brown upper parts, and is pale cream and white below, speckled with clear dark spots.

This bird lives up to its name as one of our loudest and finest songsters. Its repertoire is essentially made up of short, fluted phrases, each repeated two or more times, and usually delivered from a high perch – less musical and varied than blackbird, but equally loud. The alarm call is a sharp 'tick-tick-tick'.

Distribution and status
Widespread, but has suffered a steady decline in recent years, possibly because of the use of pesticides and also habitat loss.

Habitat preference
Woodland, parkland, meadows, heath; also gardens.

Food preference
Takes a wide range, including invertebrates, notably worms; also berries and fruits. Well known for its ability to extract the flesh from snails after bashing them against a stone 'anvil' to break the shell. A collection of broken snail shells around a hard object is a sure sign that song thrushes are around.

Redwing* W
Turdus iliacus
Redwings are slightly smaller and also darker than song thrushes, with a white stripe over the eye, and a streaked

rather than a spotted breast. The name comes from the bright red-brown flanks and inner underwing.

Redwings have a very distinctive flight call – a high-pitched 'tsweep', and flocks can be heard calling as they arrive in the autumn, often at night.

Distribution and status
A regular winter visitor from Scandinavia. Also a rare breeder, mainly in the north of Scotland.

Habitat preference
Open country such as ploughed fields, pasture, playing fields and the like; also in hedgerows (especially those with berries).

Food preference
In cold weather redwings often come into gardens to feed on berry-bearing trees or shrubs, including holly, or apples.

Mistle thrush R
Turdus viscivorus
The mistle thrush is the largest of the European thrushes. Greyer than song thrush, it also has longer wings and tail, and larger spots on the breast. The white outer tail feathers are obvious in the heavy undulating flight.

The flight call is a buzzing 'tzrrr', and the song a wild, melancholy fluting, recalling the blackbird, but with shorter, more monotonous phrases. Mistle thrushes start singing early in the season, often in February, and even during inclement weather – nearly always from a prominent position high in a tree.

This song thrush at its 'anvil' is doing its best to keep the snail population under control.

Distribution and status
Widespread, but like song thrush has suffered a steady decline in recent years.

Habitat preference
Broadleaved and coniferous woodland; wooded pasture, parkland and large gardens.

Food preference
Mainly invertebrates, but will also take berries and other fruits.

Whitethroat S
Sylvia communis
This lively warbler is one of our most attractively marked. The male has a blue-grey head, chestnut wings and white outer

Brambles offer a relatively safe nesting site for small birds such as the garden warbler.

Habitat preference
Hedgerows, scrub; not that infrequent in gardens, especially those with hedges, but often overlooked.

Food preference
Mainly insects and other invertebrates; berries in the autumn.

Garden warbler S
Sylvia borin
A rather drab, nondescript warbler, with no obvious markings – and also not easy to spot, usually remaining hidden in trees. Despite its name, the garden warbler is less common in gardens than the blackcap. The song is a rapid warble – quite musical, rather like that of blackcap, but more monotonous and lacking the final high-pitched section.

Distribution and status
Widespread in wooded areas; absent from treeless regions; commonest in the south.

Habitat preference
Tall scrub, lakeside thickets, bushy woodland margins, woods and parks, especially those with rich undergrowth such as nettles. Sometimes found in larger, wilder gardens.

Food preference
Mainly insects, spiders and the like.

tail feathers; the throat is a pure white. The female is drabber, with a brownish head. The whitethroat's song is a rapid warble, often delivered in a short flight above bushes or hedgerow.

Distribution and status
A common warbler, but its status varies according to conditions in the African wintering grounds (the Sahel regions). The population crashed in the late 1960s, and since then it has gradually recovered, but only rather slowly.

Habitat preference
Scrub, hedges, embankments, woodland edges; sometimes seen in gardens, especially if they adjoin fields.

Food preference
Insects in the breeding season; also berries in the autumn.

Lesser whitethroat S
Sylvia curruca
Rather similar to whitethroat, but without the male whitethroat's chestnut wings. One distinctive characteristic is the rather faint dark mask around the eye and cheek.

Lesser whitethroats are more secretive than common whitethroats and therefore harder to spot. But they can usually be identified by their unusual song. This begins with a very soft warble (inaudible from a distance), followed by a loud rattle, all on one note – quite unlike the song of any other native species, except perhaps the (rare and local) cirl bunting.

Distribution and status
Fairly common but secretive; absent in much of the north and south-west. Numbers tend to fluctuate.

Blackcap* S/R/W
Sylvia atricapilla
The blackcap is a common warbler, easily identified by the black (male) or chestnut-brown (female) cap. The underside is pale, and the back grey-brown.

The song of the blackcap is very pleasant, with some of the blackbird's quality, but softer and less varied. It consists of a musical warbled phrase, the last section of which rises distinctly in pitch.

Distribution and status
Blackcaps are widespread and common, with a steady increase over recent decades. They are increasingly seen overwintering, especially in mild winters. Some of these birds are probably central European blackcaps which have started spending the winter in Britain, migrating west instead of south.

Habitat preference
Open woodland, plantations, parks and gardens.

Food preference
Mainly invertebrates in spring and summer; partial to berries and fruit in autumn and winter.

Chiffchaff S/R
Phylloscopus collybita
One of our smallest warblers, with dull olive-brown plumage, a pale underside, and dark legs and feet. The chiffchaff is usually identified by the highly

The chiffchaff is a small summer visitor which likes to nest in amongst low bushes and scrub.

distinctive song that gives it its name – a monotonous, irregular repetition of two notes: 'chiff-chaff-chiff-chiff-chaff…'

Distribution and status
Widespread in areas with trees and woodland, especially in the south and south-west. Chiff chaffs are mainly summer visitors, but some stay and overwinter, especially in the south.

Habitat preference
Broadleaved and mixed woodland, parks and gardens.

Food preference
Insects and spiders, usually taken high in the trees; occasionally eats fruits in autumn and winter, although rarely visits feeders.

Willow warbler S
Phylloscopus trochilus
A small warbler with greenish-yellow plumage, the willow warbler is very similar to the chiffchaff, but usually has paler legs; the two species are hard to distinguish in the wild unless you hear them singing.

The song, however, could not be more different from the chiffchaff's: a melancholy descending series of clear notes, rising towards the end.

Distribution and status
Widespread, but its numbers have declined since the late 1980s, especially in southern England.

Habitat preference
Broadleaved and mixed woodland, parks and gardens; also fen, willow and alder scrub, and heathy birch woodland. Unlike the chiffchaff, nests among ground vegetation.

Food preference
Insects and spiders, usually taken high in the trees, and sometimes from the air.

Goldcrest R
Regulus regulus
Our smallest bird (with the closely related but rarer firecrest and the wren) – tiny, dumpy and very pretty. The male has a bright-yellow crown, edged with orange-red; the female's crown is light yellow. The plumage is olive-green above.

Goldcrests are fairly approachable but often hard to see as they typically flit about in the branches of a conifer. The song is a high-pitched, rather tinkling phrase. This bird builds a delicate nest woven into the tip of a branch, using moss, fine wool and spiders' webs.

The very similar **firecrest** (*R. ignicapillus*) has a bright-orange crown stripe and a clear black eye stripe. It is much rarer, although it does actually breed in a few southern localities.

Distribution and status
Goldcrests are widespread where there are conifers, especially in the south.

Habitat preference
Fairly closely connected with coniferous woodland, or groups of conifers in mixed woodland, parks or gardens.

Food preference
Tiny insects and spiders, usually picked from foliage.

Spotted flycatcher S
Muscicapa striata
Slim and lively, but with rather drab brown-grey plumage and a pale, streaked breast, the spotted flycatcher was once a

common sight in parks, gardens and open woodland.

This bird's feeding behaviour is really fascinating to observe. The adults tend to sit still on a prominent perch, then make repeated swooping flights to catch insects in the air. This, one of our most delightful garden birds, has sadly become very much rarer in recent years.

The charming goldcrest builds a delicate nest from moss, slung from the twigs of a conifer.

Spotted flycatchers build their nests on a ledge – either in a natural site on a branch or creeper or, as here, in a little-used garden shed.

Distribution and status
Although widespread, the spotted flycatcher has suffered a serious steady decline since the 1970s, the reasons for which are unclear. It may be due to changes in agriculture and the loss of large trees, perhaps combined with unfavourable conditions in the bird's wintering areas in southern and western Africa.

Habitat preference
Open woodland, meadows with trees, parks, churchyards and large gardens.

Food preference
Mainly flying insects; also insects picked from foliage in cool weather.

Long-tailed tit* R
Aegithalos caudatus
Very small, but with a long, narrow tail that makes up more than half its total length, the long-tailed tit has a distinctive lollipop-like appearance, especially in flight. The plumage is mainly black and white above, and pale white and pink beneath.

Long-tailed tits travel about in family groups, and in flocks in winter, sometimes mixing with other tits. They usually keep up constant high-pitched contact calls when moving about. Communal roosts are common, especially in cold weather. These birds are noted for their beautifully crafted oval nests, which incorporate feathers, moss, lichens and spiders' webs.

Distribution and status
Widespread and generally common.

Habitat preference
Woodland with rich undergrowth; parks and gardens.

Food preference
Small insects and spiders.

The nest of the long-tailed tit is a marvellous structure – oval in shape, made of lichens, moss, feathers and hairs, and with an entrance hole at the side.

Marsh tit R
Parus palustris
A small and rather compact bird with pure-white cheeks and a glossy black cap – otherwise rather drab and grey-brown. Its most characteristic call is a sharp 'pitchoo'.

The very similar **willow tit** (*P. atricapillus*) is rarer, and tends to be found in damper habitats.

Distribution and status
Widespread, especially in the south, but numbers have decreased alarmingly in recent years, possibly as a result of competition from blue, coal and great tits.

Habitat preference
Despite the name, it likes rather dry mixed woods best. Occasional in rural gardens.

Food preference
Insects in spring and summer; also seeds and berries in autumn and winter; sometimes comes to feeders, and will take peanuts.

Coal, marsh or willow tit?

The commoner tit species are easy to identify – the **great tit** is the largest, and is boldly marked; **blue tits** are small and rather brightly coloured blue and yellow; while the **long-tailed tit**, with its tiny body and long tail, looks rather like an animated lollipop.

Less common, in increasing order of rareness, are coal, marsh and willow tits. All three of these are relatively drab, the basic plumage being grey or grey-brown. They are small birds, about the size of the blue tit, and all three have an obvious black cap.

The **coal tit** (the commonest of the three) has two white wing bars and an obvious white patch along the back of its head.

The **marsh tit** and **willow tit** are extremely similar to each other: both birds seem rather large-headed, and the black cap (no white patch) extends down the back of the neck. The marsh tit's black head can appear glossy, while that of the willow tit is dull. However, they are best separated by their calls: the marsh tit has a sharp 'pitchoo, pitchoo', while the willow tit calls with a nasal 'chay-chay-chay'.

Neither marsh nor willow tits are common garden birds, but coal tits often appear, especially if there are conifers in the vicinity.

Coal tit R
Parus ater
A small bird with mainly grey-brown plumage, except for the double wing bar and the head, which is black with white cheeks; there is also an obvious narrow white patch along the back of the head. The song is a bit like the great tit's, but thinner and weaker – 'situi-situi-situi'.

Distribution and status
Widespread and numerous, but less common than the blue or great tit.

Habitat preference
Mixed woodland, especially where conifers are to be found.

Food preference
Mainly insects and spiders, which are taken from conifer foliage. Also visits feeders in autumn and winter. Coal tits tend to pick off items of food, then fly back to the safety of the trees in order to eat them. They also store food for use in hard times.

Right *You may be lucky enough to see a marsh tit in the garden, especially if there is woodland nearby. This one has brought food to its nest-hole.*

Far right *Nylon mesh bags filled with peanuts are some of the cheapest bird feeders, and are very popular with blue tits. Be sure to check the birds don't get their feet trapped, especially when the bag becomes loose.*

Blue tit* R
Parus caeruleus

As one of our commonest and prettiest garden birds, the blue tit hardly needs describing. It is a small bird with blue-and-yellow plumage, and can be quite bold and aggressive at bird tables and feeding stations. It often uses nest boxes.

Distribution and status
Widespread and common throughout.

Habitat preference
Broadleaved and mixed woodland, especially with oak; also common in parks and gardens.

Food preference
Insects and spiders; also very keen on peanuts, fat-balls, seed and other scraps. Often the first bird to visit a new feeding station.

Great tit* R
Parus major

The largest of our tit species, the great tit (pictured overleaf) is very common, and unlikely to be absent from any garden. It is easily recognisable, with a black-and-white head, a green back, yellow underparts and a broad (male) or narrow (female) black stripe down the centre of the belly.

The song is varied – often a simple repeated 'tea-cher, tea-cher...' – starting very early in the year. Great tits often uses nest boxes, and they are regular visitors to bird tables and peanut feeders.

Distribution and status
Widespread and common.

Habitat preference
Broadleaved and mixed woodland; also common in parks and gardens.

Food preference
Insects, especially caterpillars; spiders; wide range of offered food – peanuts, fat, seeds.

Male and female great tits are similar but not identical in appearance. The broad black band on the belly of this bird shows that it is a male.

Nuthatch R
Sitta europaea
This rather odd-looking bird is dumpy and woodpecker-like, with a short tail and a powerful, chisel-shaped bill. It is blue-grey above, and creamy yellow or rusty beneath.

Nuthatches are very agile and can climb up, across or even down tree branches and trunks with ease. Their loud, liquid calls are distinctive – 'tvit-vit-vit-vit'.

They nest in natural tree cavities or old woodpecker holes, reducing the entrance size to exclude larger species by daubing the edges with mud until the required diameter is achieved.

Distribution and status
Widespread and increasing in numbers, especially in the

Nuthatches feed mainly from the bark of trees, but will also come to nut and fat feeders, mainly in the winter months.

south, but not so common in less wooded areas.

Habitat preference
Mainly broadleaved and mixed woodland, parks and gardens. Nuthatches are especially fond of old trees, especially oak.

Food preference
Mainly insects, but they also take nuts and seeds from feeders and tables, especially in cold weather.

Treecreeper R
Certhia familiaris
A small, rather mouse-like bird like a miniature woodpecker, with a thin, curved bill, highly camouflaged upper parts and a pale creamy underside.

Treecreepers climb in spirals up tree trunks, searching carefully for insects and other invertebrates on and under the bark. When they reach the top of the trunk, they typically fly down to the base of an adjacent tree and start the whole climbing process again.

The call and song are high-pitched and not very easy to hear. Treecreepers nest in crevices beneath tree bark, or sometimes in specially designed boxes.

Jays have a particular liking for nuts, especially acorns, which they bury in large quantities to provide a stock for winter.

Distribution and status
Common and widespread, but easily overlooked.

Habitat preference
Broadleaved and mixed woodland, with lower numbers in coniferous woods and plantations. Also found in mature parks and large gardens.

Food preference
Small insects and spiders.

Jay R
Garrulus glandarius
This colourful member of the crow family is rather large and somewhat plump. In flight it is conspicuous, with its black tail, white rump and white-and-blue wing patches. The rest of the body is a cinnamon or pinkish colour.

Jays make a series of raw, screeching calls and can be extremely noisy, especially as they often move about in small groups.

Distribution and status
Common and widespread.

Habitat preference
Mixed woodland, wooded parks and large gardens.

Food preference
Jays take a very wide range of food, including nuts (especially acorns), insects, fruit, and also the eggs and nestlings of other birds. They have a habit of storing food in the autumn – burying acorns, for example, some of which get forgotten and then germinate, thus helping oak regeneration.

Magpie* R
Pica pica
This bird is quite unmistakable with its bold black-and-white markings and long, graduated tail. Magpies are noisy and sociable birds, often going around in groups and making loud chattering calls.

Magpies have often been accused of causing the recent decline in songbird populations, but although they do raid other birds' nests and eat eggs and nestlings, there is no actual evidence that such losses affect songbird numbers.

The magpie's nest is highly unusual, being large and made predominantly of sticks, with a loose, domed roof constructed over the top.

Distribution and status
Common and widespread, with a steady increase over recent years. Magpies are seen most frequently in the south and south-west.

Habitat preference
Magpies like open country with hedges and grassland, woodland margins, and also parks and gardens.

Food preference
A wide range of different items, including insects, fruits and seeds, eggs and nestlings, and also scraps.

65

Originally cliff and tree-hole nesters, jackdaws commonly nest in old-style chimney pots.

Jackdaw* R
Corvus monedula

Jackdaws are small and crow-like, with mainly black plumage, grey on the nape and the back of the head, and a pale eye. They are highly social birds, often nesting in loose colonies around chimneys, and also on cliffs and tall buildings, and in old trees. In winter jackdaws frequently form mixed flocks with rooks. Their calls are varied, but mostly strident and cackling.

Distribution and status

Common and widespread, with an increase over the last 20 years.

Habitat preference

Old, broadleaved woodland, cliffs (including coastal sites), quarries, parkland with old trees, churches, ruined buildings, chimneys.

Food preference

A very wide range, including scraps put out in gardens.

Rook R
Corvus frugilegus

This familiar member of the crow family is often confused with the carrion crow, but adult birds have a pale bill with a bare, pale base, and shaggy 'trousers' at the base of the legs. Rooks nest in colonies, and are noisy and very sociable, making loud and varied raucous calls.

Distribution and status

Rooks are widespread and common in lowland areas. Rookeries vary in size from just a few to a hundred or more pairs. They tend to stick to traditional sites – ideally in tall

Rooks sometimes hunt for worms and grubs on the lawn, which they patrol with a comical waddling gait.

trees or in woodland next to open fields.

Habitat preference
Open, cultivated country and woodland edges – and also in suburban areas with trees and parkland or farmland nearby. However, not very often seen in gardens.

Food preference
Mainly grain; also invertebrates such as insect larvae and worms.

Carrion crow R
Corvus corone
An all-black crow with a black bill – about the same size as a rook, but lacking the rook's 'trousers'. Crows nest in solitary pairs, not in colonies. The call is a monotonous, repeated cawing.
   The carrion crow is replaced in north and north-west Scotland, and in Ireland, by the **hooded crow**, which has a grey body.

Distribution and status
Widespread and common; populations have increased in recent years.

Habitat preference
Open country, from heathland to light woodland, parks, gardens and urban areas.

Food preference
Will eat almost anything, from seeds, invertebrates, eggs and nestlings, to scraps of all kinds. Frequently to be found foraging in gardens.

Rook or crow?
Many people use the terms 'rook' and 'crow' loosely and interchangeably. Although they may look similar, especially from a distance, there are many differences between rooks and crows.

Britain has one species of crow – the **carrion crow**, which has jet-black plumage. Note, however, that this is replaced in northern and western Scotland, and in Ireland, by the **hooded crow**, which is usually regarded as a subspecies of carrion crow. Hooded crows have a pale-grey body, the black being restricted to the head and neck, wings and tail. Some intermediate types may be seen where the subspecies meet. Carrion (and hooded) crows are solitary nesters, constructing a stick nest in a tall tree or similar site.

Rooks, on the other hand, are colonial birds, breeding in small or large rookeries made up of many nests built quite close together in the treetops. Seen close up, rooks have a pale patch at the base of the grey bill, whereas the bill of the carrion crow is black, with no pale area. Rooks also have shaggy 'trousers' at the base of their legs.

The calls are different too: carrion crows utter a simple 'kaar', repeated a couple or several times; rooks make a wider range of cawing and varied raucous sounds.

Starling* R/W
Sturnus vulgaris
The starling is one of our commonest and most familiar garden birds. It is found almost everywhere – around houses, and in woodland and open countryside.
   Dumpy in shape, and with a rather long, slender bill (see photo overleaf), starlings are adept at exploiting a wide range of habitats and opportunities. The plumage is a glossy green in spring, becoming spotted white in winter.

In autumn and winter, starlings gather into flocks and converge on a favoured roosting site. Flock members occasionally perform synchronised aerobatic manoeuvres.

Distribution and status
Widespread and very common, especially around houses and gardens. However, starlings have declined markedly in many rural areas, along with many other once common birds, probably due to agricultural 'improvements'.

67

Habitat preference
Woods, fields, parks, gardens.

Food preference
Starlings are one of the most frequent visitors to bird tables and gardens. This 'all-purpose' bird can feed on almost anything – insects, worms, scraps, fruit, berries, and even flying ants and other aerial insects, caught in circling flight.

When feeding on grubs and worms from a lawn, starlings often plunge their beaks into the soil, then open their mandibles to enlarge the hole – a rather different strategy from that of thrushes and blackbirds.

House sparrow* R
Passer domesticus
Everyone knows the humble house sparrow, which needs little introduction, although this

Above *Starlings seem able to exploit almost all sources of food, and are regular garden visitors.*

Below *Though the house sparrow has suffered declines in many cities, few gardens are without this cheeky little bird. With its black bib and grey crown, the male is more boldly marked than the female.*

species is generally much less common than previously. The male has a grey cap and a black chin, while females and young birds are a drab grey-brown. The song, is undistinguished – a rather tuneless chirping.

House sparrows usually nest in loose colonies, building untidy nests. They sometimes use nest boxes, including those built for blue tits (although the sparrows can be easily excluded by a narrow, blue-tit-sized entrance hole).

The similar **tree sparrow** (*P. montanus*) has a bright-chestnut head, and a white cheek with a black spot. It is not often seen in gardens, and is much rarer.

Distribution and status

Widespread, but commonest in the east, house sparrows (and tree sparrows) have suffered a marked decline in recent years. This phenomenon is as yet unexplained, but is perhaps due to 'cleaner' practices whereby less grain and other food is left lying around.

Habitat preference

Houses in cities, towns and villages; farmyards.

Food preference

Insects in summer, and also grain, especially in winter. House sparrows are regular visitors to bird feeders, and take many scraps.

House, tree or hedge sparrow?

We have two species of true sparrow – house sparrow and tree sparrow, and of these the house sparrow is much the commoner. **Tree sparrows** are not likely to be seen in gardens – indeed they have become quite rare anywhere in recent times. So the main potential confusion is between house sparrows and so-called hedge sparrows.

The latter species is more accurately known as the **dunnock** – a name that helps to keep its identity separate from the true sparrows. In fact it is more closely related to the robin than to the true sparrows.

House sparrows are rather dumpy, and bold, noisy and somewhat aggressive in behaviour, whereas dunnocks lead a rather secretive life, creeping about on the ground to feed. Note also the thin bill of the dunnock, combined with plumage that looks dull from a distance. In fact the dunnock's plumage, when seen at close quarters, is an intricate mixture of speckles and shades of brown and grey, but it has no bold markings, such as the black bib and white cheek of the (male) house sparrow. The bill of the house sparrow is broad and deep, like that of a finch.

House sparrows commonly feed at bird tables, and can also cling to suspended nut feeders, in the manner of green-finches. In fact, young greenfinches are quite likely to be confused with female or young house sparrows, since they have a comparable body and bill shape, and often behave in a similar fashion.

Chaffinch* R/W

Fringilla coelebs

The chaffinch (pictured overleaf) is our commonest finch, and a regular bird in gardens.

The male in the breeding season has a blue-grey crown, a brown back and a pinkish breast. The female is olive-brown above and grey-brown below. In flight, chaffinches show a clear white wing patch and bar, and white outer tail feathers.

The chaffinch's song is a pleasant, descending cadence that accelerates towards the end. Its rhythm has been likened to that of a cricket bowler running up to the crease and then finally delivering the ball with a flourish.

Distribution and status

Common and widespread; numbers have increased in recent years.

The chaffinch is one of our commonest garden birds. Here a male chaffinch is taking food from a post.

Habitat preference
Woodland, heathland, parks and gardens; flocks to fields in winter.

Food preference
Mainly insects in spring and summer; also seeds and berries in autumn and winter. Regular at bird tables.

Bullfinch R/(W)
Pyrrhula pyrrhula
This large, rather dumpy finch has a clear white rump. The male has bright rose-red under-parts, a blue-grey back, and a black head and tail, while the female is a dull brown-grey. The bullfinches call is a rather feeble whistle.

Bullfinches eat many buds, including those of fruit trees. They are therefore attracted to orchards, where they can sometimes become rather a nuisance.

Distribution and status
Widespread, but has suffered a steep decline since the mid-1970s, possibly due to the loss of trees and hedgerows, or seed-bearing weeds.

Habitat preference
Woodland, scrub, parks, gardens and orchards.

Food preference
Mainly seeds; also insects and buds.

Greenfinch* R
Carduelis chloris
This large yellow-green or brownish finch is seldom absent from the garden. It shows bright-yellow wing and tail

Bullfinches are rather shy and somewhat irregular garden visitors. The male is boldly marked with pink underparts, jet-black head and pure-white rump.

The deep, powerful bill of the greenfinch enables it to feed on a wide range of hard seeds, grains and nuts.

patches, especially in flight. The females and young are less brightly coloured, and can look rather sparrow-like. The calls and song contain characteristic wheezy, nasal notes.

Distribution and status
Very common and widespread.

Habitat preference
Mixed woodland, farmland, heaths, hedgerows, parks, orchards and gardens.

Food preference
Mainly seeds, but also insects. Greenfinches often visit bird tables and feeders. They are particularly fond of peanuts, and for a large finch are surprisingly adept at clinging to hanging nut containers.

Siskin R/W
Carduelis spinus
This very small, dainty finch is mainly green and yellow, with dark wings and a bright-yellow wing bar. The male has a black crown and a small black chin patch. The female is greyer, more streaked, and lacks the black on the head.

In gardens, siskins are generally relatively scarce

The male siskin looks rather like a miniature dark greenfinch. Siskins feed on the seeds from birch catkins and alder cones, but will also peck fragments from peanuts.

winter visitors. There are some years when they show up in gardens quite often, and visit bird tables and hanging feeders – but they are by no means regular.

Distribution and status
Local, mainly breeding in conifer plantations; variable numbers in winter.

Habitat preference
Spruce forests and conifer plantations; birch and alder trees, especially in winter.

Food preference
Small seeds and insects, often gathered from spruce, alder or pine. Fond of peanuts, especially in red feeders - perhaps because they resemble cones.

Goldfinch* R/S/W
Carduelis carduelis

Surely one of the most attractive of our garden birds, the goldfinch is a beautifully coloured small finch, with black-and-yellow wings and a bright-red face.

These birds can usually be seen flitting about in flocks, uttering pleasant, tinkling contact flight calls. The song is a rapid sequence of twittering, jingly notes.

Distribution and status
Widespread and common, particularly in lowland areas. Breeding birds tend to migrate south in the winter, but they are replaced to some extent by other birds arriving from further north.

Thistle heads should be left to go to seed as these will tend to attract goldfinches into the garden.

Habitat preference
Hedges, fields, heathland, parks, orchards and gardens.

Food preference
Eats mainly small seeds such as those of thistles, teasel and other weeds, but also insects. Goldfinches are common visitors to bird feeders, where they are especially fond of niger seed.

Linnet R/S
Carduelis cannabina

An active, somewhat modestly coloured finch – mainly brown, though the male has a red forehead and breast in the breeding season. Linnets have a twittering flight call and quite a musical, rather canary-like song.

Distribution and status
Linnets were once much more common than now, but their numbers have declined steadily since the late 1960s, probably on account of the reduced availability of weed seeds in agricultural areas.

Habitat preference
Open, cultivated country, hedgerows, heathland, parks and gardens. Nowadays not a very common garden bird.

Food preference
Insects in spring and summer; mainly seeds during the rest of the year.

Common redpoll R/W
Carduelis flammea

A very small finch with grey-brown streaked plumage, a red forehead, a small black bib and a pale double wing bar. The calls are rapid and somewhat nasal and buzzing.

Distribution and status
Common redpolls are rather local and have declined in population since the 1980s, but numbers vary and are swelled at times by migrants from further north.

Habitat preference
Heath and wooded fens; mixed woodland and plantations.

Food preference
Insects in summer; mostly seeds during the winter. In gardens, redpolls are most likely to be seen in birch or alder trees.

Yellowhammer R
Emberiza citrinella

A pretty, long-tailed bunting. The male has a bright-yellow head and a cinnamon-coloured rump; the female is duller and more streaked.

The song, which is very characteristic, is often rendered as 'a little bit of bread and no cheese' – all roughly on one note, except for the final syllable, which is pitched lower.

Distribution and status
Widespread but, in common with several other farmland birds, there has been a marked decline since the 1980s.

This male yellowhammer is bringing grubs to the nest to feed its hungry young.

The female and young birds are a dull streaked brown. The song is a rather weak, lilting phrase.

The male reed bunting is a striking bird, with its bold black head and obvious white collar.

Distribution and status
Widespread, but has declined since the 1970s.

Habitat preference
Open country with hedges and copses; heathland; bushy woodland margins.

Habitat preference
Breeds in wetlands such as reedbeds and fenland, river banks, ditches and damp willow scrub.

Food preference
Mainly insects in the breeding season; seeds and berries in autumn and winter. May feed in gardens, especially during harsh winter weather.

Food preference
Mainly seeds, including those of various grasses. Reed buntings may sometimes be seen in gardens during harsh winter weather, when they occasionally visit bird tables.

Reed bunting R
Emberiza schoeniclus
The breeding male has a black head, chin and throat, with a white collar and moustache.

Threats and dangers

Birds face many threats and dangers in their natural habitats, ranging from cold, famine and disease, to direct predation from other birds, mammals and sometimes even snakes. But the greatest threat to bird species undoubtedly comes from people – mainly indirectly from changes we have made to the landscape, and in particular the reductions to natural and semi-natural habitats.

This has happened in many different ways:

- industrial pollution of rivers and of the soil
- excessive use of pesticides and other agricultural chemicals
- removal of hedgerows, and the felling of woods and forests
- conversion of heathland, pasture and meadows either to more intensive farmland or for housing, road schemes and the like.

All of these factors have encroached upon nature and reduced bird diversity and populations.

Some of the biggest changes have been to the agricultural countryside, which has steadily become more intensive and efficient, with consequent negative impacts on the bird life. Species such as lapwings, corn buntings, skylarks, yellow

A metal girdle surrounding the trunk of a tree is a very effective way of preventing cats from approaching a nest box.

This cat deterrent has a sensor that detects movement, then emits a high-pitched sound that is inaudible to humans but disliked by cats.

wagtails and even house sparrows have suffered a decline in population.

Predators

One result of this is that gardens have become ever more important, offering food-rich oases for those birds that are able to make use of them. However, dangers of a different kind lurk there too – not least in the shape of the domestic cat.

Cats are not natural predators of garden birds, but many cats are instinctive killers and take large numbers of birds, especially fledglings, which can be very distressing. Estimates put the numbers of cats in the UK at over 7 million, and few gardens are without them.

Various devices are available to deal with the cat problem, but if you have a birding cat, try to make sure it is well fed, and keep it indoors at times of highest risk to the birds, especially in spring and early summer. A hungry cat is quite capable of clearing a nest of all its contents, killing or eating all the baby birds, or of catching them as they make their first uncertain forays.

Small bells and sonic devices are now available, and these have been shown to be quite effective in alerting birds to a nearby hunting cat.

If the offending predators come from elsewhere in the neighbourhood, there are various ways of keeping them away, whether by installing physical barriers to prevent them reaching the birds, or by means of sonic devices that deter them from approaching altogether.

Native predators, such as magpies and sparrowhawks take a toll as well, but their impact on garden bird populations is minimal – though the sight of a hawk seizing a bird from the garden may be disturbing. As has already been noted elsewhere, good numbers of sparrowhawks indicate that the songbird population is also healthy.

Grey squirrels

Another animal that impacts on garden birds is the grey squirrel. Agile and cunning, grey squirrels are attracted to the free food at bird tables, and they are surprisingly clever at climbing onto hanging feeders as well. With their sharp teeth they are quite capable of biting through the plastic cap of a hanging bird feeder in order to get at the peanuts inside.

Various tricks can be used to outwit squirrels, such as dangling the feeders from a high clothes line, or mounting them onto a thin, greased pole. Several commercial products are also available, including pole collars, and special squirrel-proof nut and seed holders (see overleaf).

This feeder is surrounded by a sturdy metal cage that will prevent squirrels and larger birds from getting at the food.

Grey squirrels also raid nests and take eggs and nestlings, but such incidents usually go unnoticed and probably do not affect garden bird numbers significantly.

Some people find squirrels and their feeding antics fascinating, and therefore do not begrudge them their share of the pickings. One way of keeping them away from a bird table is to provide an alternative source of food. It is even possible to buy squirrel mazes, which set puzzles for the squirrels to solve as they search for food.

Plate glass

Large windows or glass doors can be a hazard for garden birds, and thousands of birds perish every year by colliding in flight with solid glass. Sometimes a bird is merely stunned and may survive, but often such collisions are fatal. If the bird seems concussed, keep it in a quiet dark place until it recovers, then set it free again.

Usually these accidents happen because the bird can see light shining through from a further window and assumes that it can fly straight through an open space. Thoughtful shading with curtains or blinds can solve this, and bird silhouettes stuck to the glass may also help (see opposite).

Weather

The weather can also be a threat to garden birds. Extremely cold weather can be lethal for many resident birds, and this is where bird-friendly gardens with good supplies of water and nourishing food can be vital.

Resident species such as wrens, goldcrests and kingfishers are particularly vulnerable to prolonged bouts of cold weather. Their bodies are small, which means that they lose heat very rapidly. In the case of kingfishers, if ponds and streams freeze over, they have fewer feeding sites, and some may then move in desperation to the coast, although many will sadly perish.

The RSPB recommends feeding regularly during the winter, with high calorie seed mixes (sunflower seeds are particularly nutritious), fat, grated cheese and soaked dried fruit (see also pages 25–27).

Silhouettes and other cut-outs can be used on large, bright windows to prevent birds colliding with the glass.

Useful information

Bird organizations

The Royal Society for the Protection of Birds (RSPB)

The Lodge
Sandy
Bedfordshire
SG19 2DL
Tel. 01767 680551
www.rspb.org.uk

Europe's largest wildlife conservation charity, supported by over 1 million members, the RSPB has over 160 nature reserves, covering in total more than 275,000 ha (1,000 sq mi). The Society also produces much very useful information about garden birds and how to encourage them.

The British Trust for Ornithology (BTO)

The Nunnery
Thetford
Norfolk
IP24 2PU
Tel. 01842 750050
Fax: 01842 750030
www.bto.org

The British Trust for Ornithology is an independent scientific research trust that investigates the populations, movements and ecology of wild birds in the British Isles.

Volunteers of all ages, and from all walks of life, put their bird-watching skills to good use via the BTO. They record wild birds systematically using survey methods developed by BTO scientists, who then compile the records and analyse them for publication. This work makes a direct and vital contribution to bird conservation, by enabling both campaigners and decision-makers to set priorities and target resources. It also provides a unique insight into the state of our environment and how it may actually be changing.

BTO volunteer surveys vary in complexity and in the skills required. Even beginners can record the common birds in their own gardens (see Garden BirdWatch Project overleaf). Other surveys require the identification of all birds, heard as well as seen, on a survey plot that may be a few miles from home. Some BTO volunteer nest recorders obtain information of great importance from a single nest box, while others make annual expeditions to remote seabird colonies or undertake hair-raising climbs to treetop-nesting raptors – all on their own initiative.

Volunteers can also learn how to catch wild birds harmlessly and mark them with uniquely numbered leg rings (a period of training is required with a BTO-licensed ringer operating in their area). This makes a vital contribution to our understanding of how birds' survival rates, breeding success and movements may be changing.

The Garden BirdWatch Project

This scheme is run by the BTO in conjunction with CJ WildBird Foods Ltd. It is co-ordinated from the BTO headquarters at Thetford in Norfolk. The most important part of Garden BirdWatch is the network of volunteers who send in information on all the birds that use their gardens.

The BTO provides all the material that participants need to submit their observations, to analyse and interpret the results, and to provide feedback and answer queries. This is achieved through regular correspondence, the production of a quarterly magazine and use of the internet.

The tremendous success of Garden BirdWatch has been achieved through the relationship between amateur ornithologists and the small team of professionals in the Garden BirdWatch office. It is a great example of how people with a general interest in wild birds can work with scientists in collecting important information about the changing fortunes of garden birds.

The BTO/CJ Garden BirdWatch is a year-round project that gathers important information on how different species of birds use gardens and how this use changes over time. Gardens are an important habitat for many wild birds, providing a useful refuge for those that have been affected by the many changes in the management of our countryside.

Some 16,500 participants currently take part in Garden BirdWatch, sending in simple weekly records of the bird species that use their gardens. This information is submitted either on paper count forms or by using Garden BirdWatch Online. Each participant also supports the project financially through an annual contribution of £12. In return, they receive the quarterly colour magazine *Bird Table*, count forms and access to advice on feeding and attracting garden birds.

More details of this scheme are available on the BTO website: www.bto.org/gbw.

The Wildlife Trusts (WT)

The Kiln
Waterside
Mather Road
Newark
Nottinghamshire
NG24 1WT
Tel. 0870 036 7711

This is a partnership of 47 local WildlifeTrusts, and is in fact the largest UK charity that is exclusively dedicated to conserving all our habitats and species. Altogether they have a membership of more than 530,000.

More than 2,500 sites in the UK are cared for as nature reserves by the Wildlife Trusts. Together, they cover over 80,000 ha (300 sq mi) and include habitats of all types, from woods and meadows to mountains and moorlands, and from ponds and rivers to cliffs and beaches. Many are provided with information centres, leaflets and signs. Most of these nature reserves are open to the public.

The Wildlife Trusts also promote wildlife-friendly gardening.

Garden bird food suppliers

There are now several specialist suppliers of food and other materials for garden birds, including those companies listed opposite. However, it is also worth trying one of your local garden centres, as most of them supply birdfood, nest boxes and the like.

CJ WildBird Foods Ltd
The Rea
Upton Magna
Shrewsbury
SY4 4UR
Tel. 01743 709555
Fax: 01743 709504
www.birdfood.co.uk

Ernest Charles
Copplestone
Crediton
Devon
EX17 2YZ
Freephone: 0800 731 6770
Fax: 01363 84147
www.ernest-charles.com

Garden Bird Supplies Limited
Wem
Shrewsbury
SY4 5BF
Tel. 01939 232233
Fax: 01939 233155
www.gardenbird.com

The Bird Table
Laindon Road
Horndon-on-the-Hill
Essex
SS17 8QB
Tel. 01268 413109
Fax: 01268 419258
www.thebirdtable.co.uk

Further Reading

The CD-ROM Guide to Garden Birds
BirdGuides, 2002

Robert Burton
The RSPB New Bird Feeder's Handbook
Dorling Kindersley, 2000

Dominic Couzens
The Secret Lives of Garden Birds
Christopher Helm, 2004

Dominic Couzens and Mike Langman
The Pocket Guide to Garden Birds
Mitchell Beazley, 1999

Paul Doherty
The DVD Guide to Common and Garden Birds
Bird Images Video Guides, 2004

Chris du Feu
The BTO Nestbox Guide
BTO, 2003

Mark Golley
The Birdwatcher's Pocket Field Guide to Birds of Parks and Gardens
New Holland Publishers, 2004

Mark Golley, Stephen Moss and David Daly
The Complete Garden Bird Book
New Holland, 1996

N. Matthews
Garden For Birds
Chalksoft, 1992

Stephen Moss
Collins Gem Guide: Garden Birds
Harper Collins, 2004

Stephen Moss
Collins Wild Guide: Garden Birds
Harper Collins, 2005

Stephen Moss and David Cottridge
How to Attract Birds to your Garden
Silverdale Books, 2003

Detlef Singer
Collins Nature Guide: Garden Birds of Britain and Europe
Harper Collins, 1996

Index

Italic refers to pictures

alder 12
ash 12, *37*

beech 12
birch 12
bird cake, home-made 27
bird cherry 12
bird food suppliers 78
bird tables *24*, *25*, *26*, 28
birdbath 18
blackbird 55, *56*
blackcap 59
blue tit 63, *63*
books on birds 79
bramble 12
British Trust for Ornithology 77
bullfinch 70, *70*
butterfly, tortoiseshell *21*

chaffinch 69, *70*
cherry tree 12
chiffchaff 59, *59*
coal tit 62
cotoneaster 16
crabapple *11*, 13
crows 67
cuckoo 46
cypress, Lawson 16

dangers to birds 74-7
directory of birds 40-75
dove 45-6
dunnock *53*, 54

elder 13
excluders 29, 76

fat foods 27
feeders 28-31, *29*, *76*
feeding birds 21-31
fieldfare 55, *55*
firethorn *15*, 16
foods for birds 25-7, 78
fountain 19, *19*
flycatcher, spotted 60, *60*

Garden BirdWatch scheme 33, 78
garlic mustard *9*
glass, protection from 76
goldcrest 60, *60*
goldenrod 16
goldfinch 72, *72*
great tit 63, *64*

greenfinch 70, *71*
guelder rose 13
gulls 44

hawthorn 13
hazel 13
heron, grey 41, *41*
holly *12*, 13
honeysuckle 13
hornbeam 13
house martin 50, *51*
household scraps 27
Hydrangea petiolaris 16
hygiene 33

insect-eating birds 22
introduction 4-6
ivy 13, *13*

jackdaw 66, *66*
jay 65, *65*

kestrel *39*, 43
kingfisher 48, *48*

large garden layout *8*
lawns 17-18, *17*
linnet 72
live food 26-7
logs *10*
long-tailed tit 61, *61*

magpie 65
mallard 42
marsh tit 62, *63*
meadow 17, *18*
mealworms 27
Michaelmas daisy 16
mistle thrush 57
moorhen 43, *43*
nest boxes 34-7, *34*, *35*, *36*, *37*, 74
nesting sites *37*, 38-9, *38*, *39*
niger seed 26
nuthatch *24*, 64, *64*

oak 14
owls 46, 47-8, *47*

parakeet, ring-necked 46
peanuts 25
pigeons 45, *45*
pine, Scots 14
planning 9-20
pond 18-19, *19*, *20*
predators 75

reading matter 79
redwing 56
reed bunting 73, *73*

references 77-9
resident birds 40
robin *24*, *26*, 54, *54*
rook 66, *66*
rose, wild 14, *14*, *22*
rowan 14, *14*
Royal Society for the Protection of Birds 77

sea buckthorn 12
seed-eating birds 23
seeds for birds 26
shrubs 10-16
silhouettes on glass 77
siskin 71, *71*
small garden layout 7
song thrush *21*, 56, 57
sparrowhawk 42, *42*
sparrows 68-69, *68*
squirrels 75
starling 67, *68*
summer feeding 31
summer visitors 40
sunflower 16, *16*
sunflower seeds 26
swallow 50, *50*, 51
swift 50

teasel 14, *23*
thistle 15
thrushes 55-7
tits 61-3, *61*, *63*, *64*
traveller's joy 15
treecreeper 64
trees 10-16

wagtails 52, *52*
warblers 57-9, *58*, *59*
water features 18-20
waxwing *52*, 53
wayfaring tree 15
weather 76
whitethroats 57-8
wild cherry 12
wild rose 14, *14*
Wildlife Trusts 78
willow 15
winter feeding 31-2
winter visitors 40
wisteria 16
woodpeckers 48-9, *49*
woodpigeon 45, *45*
wren 53, *53*

yellowhammer 72, *73*
yew 15